Site 18

Short stories from an isolated Air Force
radar detachment in Japan
during the Korean War and the Cold War.

Richard E. Waldron

Squantum Publishing Company
54 Monmouth Street
Quincy, Massachusetts 02171
USA

Site 18

**Short stories from an isolated Air Force
radar detachment in Japan
during the Korean War and the Cold War.**

copyright 2005

by
Richard E. Waldron

ISBN: 0-9656593-7-2

Library of Congress Control Number: 2005902095

SAN: 299-3465

Squantum Publishing Company
54 Monmouth Street
Quincy, Massachusetts 02171
USA

**cover photo: SCR-270 radar at sunset:
Sandy Friedman**

Printed in the United States by Morris Publishing • Kearney, NE 68847

to: Polly

and

to anyone who ever served on
an isolated Air Force radar site –

especially in Northern Japan.

Acknowledgements

I'll take the blame for any of the writing and I'll spread the blame around for some other stuff.   ...but seriously folks - I had help in checking facts, filling in blanks, supplying old photographs and producing newspaper articles. They added to my own shoebox of stories, letters and photos of my time at Site 18 and Misawa AB.

For the help received from others I gratefully acknowledge:

Photographs
Bob Cole: Nashville reunion group
Sandy Friedman: **front book cover;** horseback inspection
Reno Giuntoli: bald heads
Tony Ocampo: mess hall ladies
Al Setting: Mohawk haircuts
Carlos Tidwell: dancing the tonka-bushi

Facts
horses: Larry Charbonneau, Arlie Jensen, Frank Watanabe //
radio message: Dick Loose // Teshio: Tony Ocampo //
twins: Paul Markovich // misc. Bob Coblentz, Art Freihoefer,
Sandy Friedman, Dixie Howell, Red Rife, Carlos Tidwell //

Newspaper Articles
Red Rife
Jim Gover and Jim Maddock (Site 26, Nemuro)

Alumni Names and Jobs
Tim Dunne, Sandy Friedman, Dick Loose,
Tony Ocampo, Al Setting, Carlos Tidwell
Major Haines (deceased) - Haines' Rangers list of the 1960's
511th Reunion Assoc. list - Don Simmons, Roger Wolf, others

Preface

This book, *Site 18*, took over fifty years to complete.

In fact, it would not be finished yet if it were not for the nagging of a few friends and relatives who read a couple of stories I had written and asked if I was going to write a book. (Well, ok, maybe they only mentioned it in passing and didn't really nag me.)

So if you have any complaints, blame them. Start with Al, Reno and Jim, plus Hedy, Kitty, and Polly - and my sisters Joie, Kathy and Peggy. It's their fault.

~~~

Site 18 was the name of a small Air Force radar detachment in northern Japan in the 1950's. This book, a slice of that time, it is a compilation of short stories, photographs, descriptions, newspaper articles and names of those stationed at 18 in 1952 and 1953, the time I was there. There is also a troopship story and a football story.

~~~

I finished writing this more than fifty years after the events but I don't pretend to have the memory required to write details of so long ago. But I do have a shoebox with old letters and stories written at the time. And some old photographs.

I also had the help of others from those years. They have shoe-boxes too. Their contributions, corrections and reminders helped to finally complete the book.

And I had help in listing names from the 511th AC&W (Aircraft Control & Warning) Reunion Association who have located a few thousand veterans who served on radar sites in Northern Japan in the fifties. The Association, started in 1994, has an annual reunion that is something special because it is fun to see friends from fifty years ago — even if *they* look older...

~~~

Back to the book: This is mostly about a small Air Force radar detachment far from other American bases or sites. The physical size of the site was not much more than that of a football field and the number of personnel stationed there at the time was about sixty - all enlisted men except from one-to-three officers.

I was an enlisted man, a radio operator, assigned to Site 18 right out of radio school with a classmate, and we were told that the tour of duty on a site was two-and-a-half years. That's a long time to look forward to, stuck in a tiny place out in the boonies on the other side of the world. Plus they told us stories about the terrible winters and humungous snowfall amounts which were off the chart. With that indoctrination prospects looked bleak, but much of it turned out to be fun.

~~~

Site 18 was at the top of Hokkaido, at the top of Japan. The next island, 32 miles north, was occupied by Russia who took it from Japan after WWII. As a benchmark, the distance from Site 18 to the major Japanese cities like Tokyo in southern Japan was over a thousand miles.

~~~

The mission for the radar sites during the Korean War and later in the Cold War was to give navigational aid to patrolling F-86 Sabre jets, L-20 courier planes, and RB-29 photo aircraft. The

RB-29, an ancestor to the famous U-2 spy plane, was a modified WWII bomber capable of taking pictures of Russia and Russian held islands near Japan. Thanks to two friends who sent copies, *Site 18* has verbatim accounts of published articles about RB-29 encounters with Russian MIGs and losses involved.

Beside navigational aid to American aircraft, the early warning sites were responsible for monitoring Russian air activity near Japan, over parts of Russia and over islands controlled by Russia. This observation work was continued during the Cold War by both the Americans and Japanese, and in the late 1950's the Japanese took over both the jobs and the sites.

~~~

Life was informal due to the few personnel, the remote location, and 'permission' of the one commanding officer in the beginning and the two c.o.'s who followed later during my fifteen months. Each took the approach that the military responsibilities came first. Then as long as the jobs were done efficiently and correctly then the off-duty life and events were less important or almost didn't matter. Many of us in the ranks took that approach and ran with it.

We had a good group, but there were no leaders. This may have been a result of all the rotating shift work. There were morning shifts, afternoon shifts, evening shifts, late night shifts, all-night shifts, 12-hour shifts, 24-hour shifts - and even thirty-day shifts. And a 7-day work week. Often people who worked the previous night slept during the day and so were not involved if something went on during the day. With so many different shifts, those who had time off together one day may not have the same time off together for weeks.

Regardless of the rotating and varied shifts, I think we really appreciated the laid back, somewhat non-military approach allowed on the site. We didn't have to sweat the small stuff, and I don't think we abused the privilege.

~~~

My thoughts of my two years in a foreign country 10,000 miles from home, at the know-it-all and impressionable ages of 19 and 20, are etched in my memory - at least parts of them. I do know that researching *Site 18* brought back more memories, one leading to another, and more good than bad.

I also think of the guys who were there and are dead now. There are many - too many. Some never grew old, and they remain in my memory as they were back in '52 and '53 when all of us were young, healthy, full of life, laughing and complaining about whatever, knowing everything and knowing nothing.

~~~

It's been fun rummaging through the shoebox and writing about things found there. Site life was different from life on an air base, and some thought Site 18 was more different than others. Maybe it was; I don't know. But boy, wouldn't it be fun to be 19 again.

oooooooeeeee. you betchum. hontoh. icky-mashoh. eema. hyaku.
        (for sure)   (let's go)   (now) (hurry)

Oh well. Hope you enjoy the book. If you don't, you can blame Al, Reno and Jim, and Hedy, Kitty, and Polly - and don't forget Joie, Kathy and Peggy. Like I said earlier, it's all their fault.

Dick Waldron   Quincy, MA
                                                          2005

Table of Contents

****

Short Stories

****

Descriptions

ix

Photographs

Newspaper Articles

****

Shipping Out

It was during the Korean War and there were almost 5,000 young soldiers and airmen on board the big gray troopship as it headed out of San Francisco Bay.

Most were Army personnel and a few hundred were Air Force, but the lopsided difference in numbers and inter-service rivalries were not on anyone's mind. Other thoughts took over and there was a stillness on the huge vessel as it moved slowly through the water.

The troopship was going to either Japan or Korea, or both. Exactly which, only the civilian merchant marine officers of the ship knew. None of the soldiers or airmen knew, so rumors were everywhere.

Regardless of what they thought or hoped, most were resigned in their minds to the same destination: they were shipping out to the war in Korea.

~~~

The day had begun as many had in the military, at 0400 hours. To those involved it seemed that every time a troop activity was scheduled it started in the middle of the night, bogged down, and actually got under way late morning. They figured today would be no exception.

There wasn't much packing of gear to do since it had been done leisurely the night before when the list was posted of who

1

would be shipping out the next day.

No off-base passes were issued for that evening and the young enlisted men in their teens and early twenties, many just out of high school, spent the time packing, repacking, writing letters, having a beer at the enlisted club, going to a movie without really watching it, or strolling quietly around the sprawling embarkation center.

The prevailing mood in the barracks of those on the shipping list was mostly one of quiet thoughtfulness. A few showed some nervous jocularity trying to put forth a what-the-hell-let's-go attitude. But they didn't convince anyone.

Most had been waiting for a couple of weeks to ship out and during that time the days and nights dragged.

The humdrum life of a transient enlisted man waiting to ship was filled with K.P., work details, records checks, medical checks, shots, rare off-base passes, and rumors that floated around since there was no real information available.

Because of the aggravating transient life some guys were jealous when others shipped out before them. They were anxious to get going themselves. But this was before their actual turn came.

~~~

0400 on the big day finally arrived and chow lines formed in the chilly darkness of the early California morning. They said little as they picked at their scrambled eggs, cold toast and tasteless bacon in the quiet mess hall where only the clink of silverware on the tin trays were heard.

After breakfast they shuffled back to the transient barracks to

2

throw their shaving gear and odds and ends into their duffel bags and overnight bags, one of each they were allowed to carry.

Then came the mustering formations on the drill fields in Class A dress uniforms with overstuffed duffel bags and smaller ditty bags. When their names were called they yelled out roster numbers and ship compartment numbers that had been assigned to them and then they boarded waiting busses, awkwardly handling the bulky, tube-shaped and heavy duffel bags.

Eventually a long bus caravan headed off the base for the harbor and an awaiting troopship. The cool air was invigorating as the sun peeked over the mountains, shooing the chill and mist before it.

Back in the barracks the rest of the transients not scheduled to leave were waking up, rubbing their eyes, and preparing for another dull day of processing, trivial chores, and aggravation while waiting their turn to ship out.

The bus ride took about an hour through hills, past farms, into small towns, out of small towns, and through the outskirts of San Francisco. Nothing was said on the busses, even among close friends, as they watched the farms, towns and city slowly wake up. They just stared out the windows quietly, and were stared back at quietly.

At the pier they got into formations by compartments number and relaxed, smoked, talked, swore at the Army and the Air Force, and joked as only G.I.'s can.

They griped about the red tape and the slow-moving lines boarding the huge grey monster looming before them. California weather and San Francisco fog took verbal abuse as did the transient life and the base they had just left, with many voicing complaints about the chicken discipline and aggravating attitudes

3

by the permanent party personnel that did the processing.

Compassion was mentioned, though, for the enlisted medic who had the dubious distinction of being the short-arm inspector, and the endless lines he faced every day.

The long, snaking lines of soldiers and airmen in dress uniforms with duffel bags and overnight bags at their feet moved slowly to board the ship, and it was late morning before all were aboard.

At dockside the ship seemed huge - hundreds of feet long and with the lowest deck so high that they had to crane their necks to look up and see it.

But the troopship was actually just a leftover from WWII with no special size or appearance. Probably one of dozens made in a big rush during WWII.

Some already on board lined the rails and watched the proceedings on the dock, with the arrival of dozens of busses and the loose formations and slowly moving lines of soldiers and airmen. Other first arrivals idly explored the ship by wandering around the decks.

There were two steep gangplanks which led from the dock to small openings in the side of the ship, and the gangplanks were narrow. After more checking of names, rosters and I.D.'s at the bottom of the gangplank, it was a tricky climb up the narrow steel steps of the gangplank, especially carrying the bags.

They carried their duffel bags on one shoulder held in place by one hand, and carried the overnight bags in the other hand, making the climbers awkward, top-heavy, off-balance, and unable to use the guard rail since both hands were full.

But somehow they made the steep climb into the small mouth

4

in the side of the ship that swallowed them up as they disappeared inside.

Once inside the ship directions were given by some of the advanced party of G.I.'s who had come aboard the day before. Most of the directions to the specific compartments were downward, down many flights of slippery steel stairs.

The duffel bags were heavy and cumbersome but everyone had to keep moving even as the weight seemed to get heavier and the movement more awkward. At the top of a flight of stairs they heaved their bags down and retrieved them at the bottom, where they continued along the next hallway or down the next flight of stairs.

The farther down into the hold of the ship they went, the more uncomfortable and sweaty they became in their Class A dress uniforms. Many shook their heads and swore as they became more laughingly irritable. Gripes, swearing, and nervous laughs of resignation of what they were doing mingled with the noise of their bags sliding along the steel decks and down flights of stairs.

The compartments that greeted them as their home for some unknown number of days or weeks were depressing. They were huge dimly-lit rooms filled with tiers of bunks stacked from floor to ceiling, each bunk two feet from the one above and below it.

The aisles between the rows of bunks were strewn with duffel bags and getting around them trying to find an empty bunk was slow and difficult.

But gradually everyone got themselves through the narrow passageways and found an empty bunk they would call home for the foreseeable future.

It seemed like everyone did the same thing after that: they tossed their overnight bag on the bunk, dropped their duffel bag on the deck, took off their hats, ran a sweaty forearm across their foreheads, knitted their brows, shook their heads, and swore - some even with a smile.

They had just moved into their new home.

~~~

Each compartment held a few hundred men and when in their bunks they were literally stacked on top of each other. The bunks were five high from floor to ceiling and each resident had less than two feet of vertical pace from the guy or ceiling above him.

The bottom bunk had a few inches below it to the floor, or steel deck.

These distances were reduced when the bunks were occupied and the canvas sagged. They would later find that climbing into the upper bunks required stepping on the edges of lower bunks, waking up or bothering people, and then scrunching into their own narrow space.

~~~

The bunk construction was simply canvas material stretched over metal pipes, forming a man-sized rectangle. During inspections the bunks were raised into a vertical position giving the illusion of plenty of open space in the compartment.

But it was an illusion.

Bedding consisted of two brown army blankets, one of which was used as a pillow and the other as a lower bed sheet to alleviate the coarseness of the canvas.

Most compartments had no portholes and the heat made not only the blankets superfluous but sleep would later prove difficult. Also, it was not exactly comforting to know they would be spending so much time in a crowded compartment below the water line.

Overnight bags were kept on the bunks and duffel bags piled on top of each other wherever there was room.

The narrow aisles were roomy enough for one person to pass by but with the duffel bags on the floor passage was slow and sometimes the bags had to be climbed over.

The rows of bunks, tiers of bunks, narrow aisles, the stifling heat, dim lights, and overcrowded living space made the general affect almost laughable. Later they would find conditions could get nerve-wracking during the long hours and days of inactivity during the trip across the Pacific.

Not least of which would be unsatisfying salt water showers and the lingering smell of people being seasick.

~~~

The up-coming living conditions were not completely realized at first by the newcomers, but a few veterans who had traveled previously on a troopship knew what to expect. They didn't like it but at least they were not surprised.

The first-timers were more concerned with the underlying adventure of a big troopship heading for parts unknown. Many acted like little kids or farmers in a big city for the first time. This was like nothing they had ever known or imagined, and they reacted differently. Some shrugged, some griped, some laughed, and some said nothing.

~~~

After finding an empty bunk and dropping their locked over-night bags on the bunk and their locked duffel bags on the floor, most filtered back up on deck to cool off, explore, look around at San Francisco Bay, and watch as preparations were made to get underway.

~~~

The military band on the dock played the Star Spangled Banner, a few families and girl friends cried and waved handkerchiefs, the narrow gangplanks were lowered to the dock, mooring lines were lifted off capstans by the line-handlers, dropped into the water and then hauled on board by the ship's civilian merchant marine crew.

The ship's foghorn and whistle blew four short blasts, and two tugboats pulled the vessel very slowly away from the dock. In slow motion the pier receded, the band played on, a few shoreside hand-kerchiefs continued to wave, and a curious stillness settled over the ship. Few moved or spoke.

~~~

They crowded all open parts of the decks that were not off-limits and watched silently as the ship went under the Bay Bridge, gazing in awe at its length - seven miles.

Next they watched San Francisco, City of Seven Hills, slide by quietly on the left, or port side. A cable car was seen climbing Powell Street and some smiled at this anachronism.

On the starboard side Oakland, The Twin City, was stared at and a commercial airliner was followed by hundreds of eyes as it came in low over the ocean to land at International Airport where one runway ended at the water's edge.

Alcatraz came up on the right also. It was less than a mile away from the ship and first impressions were its high grey walls and

8

stillness. One wall had huge block lettering "Cable Crossing". It looked even more foreboding with its isolation and gun towers than it seemed in its pictures. On the ship they could almost feel and see convicts watching the troopship from the prison.

Alcatraz passed to the rear, slowly, and the Presidio, a small Army base, came up on the left. Its stucco buildings with red tile roofs and many trees made it one of the more attractive bases. The walls around the Presidio reminded some of the fact that it had been a fort many years ago, built to protect San Francisco Bay against foreign invaders. No one was sure if its old cannons had ever been fired or what its function was now but it lived on as a small and active Army base.

~~~

The Golden Gate Bridge approached dead ahead in all its yellow-orange splendor - the last departure point before the Pacific Ocean, the unknown Far East, and war.

The bridge came up slowly, in plenty of time for most on board to marvel at its engineering and single span that stretched almost two miles between Marin County and San Francisco.

The troopship, its tugboats long-since gone, headed for the middle of the channel under the bridge. As the ship approached the bridge there was some concern on board that there would not be enough clearance to pass under without hitting it.

The Golden Gate at first seemed huge yet also close to the water when seen from a distance. Its yellow-gold color from the orange paint and the sun, and its overall beauty and size attracted everyone's gaze.

Their feeling was different from seeing the Golden Gate Bridge from land, in pictures or crossing over it by car. This was special; this was going under it, and the only sound was the murmur in the background of the constant throb of the ship's engines and the occasional screeching seagull.

The Golden Gate came closer, slowly. Then with the hollow sound of the rhythmic beat of the ship's engine echoing off the underside of the bridge, the troopship was under it. The clearance seemed at least a hundred feet above the top of the ship, and cars were heard up on the bridge.

From underneath, the width, the height and majesty of the bridge impressed even cynics.

~~~

Soldiers and airmen watched as the bridge receded to the rear and became part of the high cliffs and green hills that hid Marin County and San Francisco from view.

The color of the bridge wasn't as noticeable from the Pacific side since it was in the shadow of the sun, but the yellow-orange affect was still there.

Then the Golden Gate Bridge slowly slipped out of sight behind the ship, below the horizon.

~~~

The big, gray troopship was unescorted as it moved with the low throb of its engines relentlessly out to sea, and nothing was seen in the distance but ocean and sky.

Some of the young men stared off into nothingness from places on deck or while leaning on the rail.

Others slowly made their way down the steel stairs from the outside decks to their compartments, looking for the solitude of their bunks.

They didn't talk much and there was almost an eerie stillness on board as five thousand men either on deck or down in the huge overcrowded rooms were quiet.

They were lost in their own thoughts, and most did not notice the muffled hum and throb of the ship's engines in the background.

Probably like other wars with other troopships full of troops heading overseas, each man aboard wondered -

...Would he end up in Korea?

...If not Korea, where?

...How long it would take to get there?

...When would he get home again?

...Would he get back in one piece?

...Would he get back, period?

...Who here would never see the Golden Gate again ?

Each man's thoughts wandered and wondered. All anyone knew was that they were shipping out on a troopship headed into the darkness of the Pacific, toward war in Korea.

Troopship: General Weigel

The Houseboy

During the Korean War, in 1952, six of us classmates fresh out of the Air Force radio operator school in Mississippi arrived in Japan and were assigned to Misawa Air Base on Honshu.

Further processing split us up among the small Early Warning radar detachments on Hokkaido, the next Japanese island north.

On Hokkaido there were about a dozen so-called 'remote' or 'isolated sites' each many miles from the next one, small in size, small in numbers of personnel, and loaded with various radar and radio equipment.

The Table of Organization for a site was only 60 enlisted men and two officers, and the tour of duty for unmarried enlisted men, as most were, was thirty months - a long time to be stationed at a small, isolated location.

The unusual military living conditions, isolation, and the 2 ½ year tours allowed the Air Force to permit a few amenities to exist that were not permitted on regular Air Force bases.

One amenity was the hiring of local schoolboys to do individual housework and laundry for the troops. They were called houseboys.

~~~

Hiring of houseboys was optional for the troops, and if hired, the houseboys worked and were paid indirectly by whoever they were assigned to. The site interpreter hired them, collected their pay from the G.I.'s, and he paid the houseboys.

14

The cost per man for a houseboy was a thousand yen a month – about three dollars and fifty cents – and each houseboy had five to ten guys on his list to take care of.

The isolated detachment that Al and I were assigned to was Site 18 at the very top of Hokkaido, a few miles up a potted dirt road north of Wakkanai, a small fishing village. We were as far north as we could go. The next island, thirty-two miles away, could be seen and it belonged to Russia.

Site 18 was on a former Japanese coast guard station with a few permanent buildings and a fifty-foot tent for new arrivals and visitors. Personnel assigned numbered about fifty enlisted men and one officer, and the whole area was not much bigger than a football field.

Al and I were each nineteen, just arrived from radio school in the States, and neither spoke or understood a word of Japanese.

Eddie, who would turn out to be our houseboy, was about fourteen, in about the ninth grade in school, and did not speak or understand a word of English.

…Hm.   Would there be a failure to communicate?

The small number of houseboys who worked on the site were mostly young kids of junior high and high school age. Their job was simple: do the housework in the living quarters every day and do the laundry once a week for each man he was working for.

Al and I were assigned to a room with three other guys and the five of us joined in hiring Eddie to be our houseboy at the going rate of $3.50 a month – a thousand yen.

For this he made the beds, swept and mopped the floor, dusted, polished boots and shoes, changed bed linen, and once a week did each man's laundry. Eddie came in five days a week and worked two hours or so. When finished he left the site and walked into town to school.

But the language barrier remained.

Sometimes Al or I tried to talk to Eddie about some small housekeeping or laundry job. And each time we tried to combine sign language with some very basic English.

We also spoke louder because, being American, we of course believed yelling in English helped when trying to communicate with someone in their language.

Eddie would listen to us politely, smile, shake his head, and acknowledge us by saying, "wakatanai."

Then he would go about doing whatever he had been doing.

At first we assumed that was the end of it. We thought Eddie understood what either of us had said to him, and we thought that his smile and agreeable nature meant he understood.

We did not notice that when he shook his head it was the Japanese way of saying no, just as it is in English.

Because he hadn't understood.

During our first few weeks on the site we tried to talk to Eddie about little things. But we weren't getting through to him and we couldn't figure out why not.

All we could hear back from him was, "wakatanai."

To our untrained ears Al and I thought Eddie was just answering us by saying the name of the town, which was Wakkanai.

We thought that was kind of a dumb answer.

That made us think that Eddie, although a nice kid, may not have been the brightest bulb in the chandelier.

Still it didn't make sense. To us he seemed to understand and to agree to do whatever chore we said. But whatever it was did not get done. How come?

Al and I couldn't figure it out, so we decided to ask for help from Paul Sheehan – another Boston Irishman – because Paul had been at Wakkanai longer and knew some Japanese words.

Paul came with us as Al and I spoke to Eddie about some minor housekeeping or laundry thing we wanted Eddie to do. Eddie stood there and listened politely.

Naturally, we even spoke louder to make sure we were getting through.

When we finished, Eddie shook his head, smiled and said, as usual, "Wakatanai."

I turned to Paul and said, "See? See what I mean? No matter what we say to Eddie he just smiles and says 'Wakkanai', which is the name of the town. What's with this kid?"

Paul laughed and said, "No, you jerks. Eddie just said he did not understand a word of what you told him. Look, the name of the town is Wakkanai. Eddie didn't say that. He said 'wakatanai'; that means 'I don't understand'."

"Huh?"

"Sheesh, you new guys. What kind of dummies are they sending us from Misawa these days? You guys can't even tell the difference between 'Wakkanai' and 'wakatanai.'"

"I guess not," I said sheepishly.

And so Al and I learned our first Japanese words – maybe.

~~~~~~

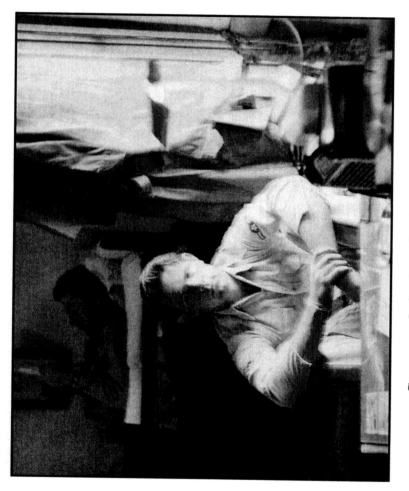

Grover wondering just what he and Slim did
to win two damn Yankees for roommates.

A Radio Message

During the Korean War the United States Air Force built and manned about a dozen small radio and radar detachments along the coasts of northern Japan as part of an aircraft control and warning system.

The small detachments were called isolated sites.

In 1952 most sites had about fifty enlisted men and one officer, and the round-the-clock mission included the monitoring by radar Russian air activity north of Japan.

Related to the radar mission was daily Morse Code radio traffic - spare parts requisitions, weather reports, arrivals and departures of personnel, and various very mundane and routine messages.

Not very exciting.

But one remote site in the far north had an attraction that caused additional radio traffic occasionally. That was the local availability of seafood delicacies. These delicacies were huge king crabs caught offshore near the site by Japanese crabfishermen.

The shellfish, a major part of the Japanese economy and famous for their size and taste, soon became a favorite of senior officers at the air base a few hundred miles south that controlled the sites.

Once the word got around, landline phone calls came to this particular site from senior officers at the home base asking that some king crabs be shipped to them as a favor.

When the requests for king crabs came in, the Commanding Officer of the site, a first lieutenant, told Frank, the Japanese interpreter, to buy the crabs and have them packed for shipping.

Then the box would be included with other items to be carried from the site to the base hundreds of miles south by a courier.

This weekly courier, a job rotated among enlisted men and a job most guys did not volunteer for, took at least three days round-trip. It involved taking military papers, old movies and outgoing mail down to the base and bringing back similar items, especially incoming mail.

If a courier's trip included crabs he was told to deliver them personally to the officer who had asked for them.

But after awhile requests for king crabs became more of an irritation and distraction to the Commanding Officer at the site. He figured he had more important things to do than ship shellfish to colonels.

The additional box of crabs was also an unwanted chore to the courier because the trip was a bit complex with its many changes among trains, taxis, military vehicles, and a ferryboat.

At each transportation change the courier had to unload his awkward combination of personal ditty bag, military official papers pouch, mail bag, movie cases and a box of crabs.

Then tote them all to the next connection and load them onto whatever means of transportation it was. This loading and unload-ing went on four or five times during the trip – and all the while the courier, carrying a .45 sidearm, sweated uncomfortably in his dress uniform.

So an additional and hardly top priority box of crabs was not welcome by both the C.O. and the couriers.

Then one particular time another request came in for some crabs and the site Commanding Officer took care of it as he had so often in the past.

He gave orders to Frank to get a box of crabs packed for shipment south, and he gave orders to Buck, the first sergeant, to volunteer a courier and have him take the crabs to Misawa and deliver them.

These orders were carried out and the courier who unexpectedly found himself volunteered left the next day.

He was dressed in his Class A dress uniform with a .45 sidearm, and was loaded down with a military pouch, mail bag, movie box, overnight bag and a box of crabs.

Jesse, the motor pool driver, drove the six-by that took the courier and his mixed load to the RTO station and then helped him load his stuff onto the old coal train.

Then Jesse drove the truck back to the site and reported to the lieutenant that the courier got on the train ok and was on his way to Misawa.

The lieutenant wrote out a departure message, gave it to one of the Morse Code radio operators on duty in the radio room next to the orderly room, and told him to send it down to headquarters.

The radioman, an Airman Second Class, scanned the routine message as usual before encoding it.

Then he stopped short.   ...It didn't look right.

He read it again. But it still didn't look right so he went back to the C.O. for clarification, saying he thought there might be a mistake.

The C.O., more interested and involved with situations more important that a courier departure, took the message, read it, gave it back, and said there was no mistake. But the radioman persisted.

He said there might be a little problem in the wording with this one. But the C.O. would have none of it and told him with a snarl to just send the damn thing as is.

As he left the orderly room the radioman still could not help wondering if this message was just an accurate statement of facts or if it was a bit tongue-in-cheek.

Did the Old Man have a trace of a smile or a twinkle in his eye when he said to send it?

...Could be. But the radioman wasn't sure.

No matter. It was to be sent. Enlisted men with two stripes did not argue with commanding officers.

So the radioman went back to the radio room where he encrypted the routine message on the code machine, flipped and dipped the transmitter, called the main base on the radio via Morse Code and tapped out the brief departure message. It included the following detail:

> Airman Second Class Smith
> departed this site today as courier
> with a case of crabs for the colonel.

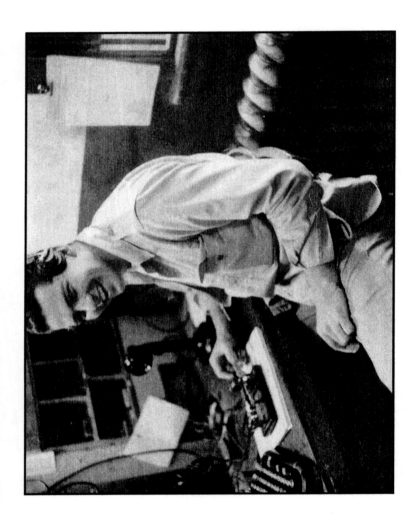

Rather informal midnight shift.

Space Cadet

Space Cadet and I first met during a radio transmission one morning in 1953 while I was on duty at the direction finding station at Site 18 in Wakkanai.

"Air Force 2783 calling Wakkanai Dog Fox. Over."

"Roger, Air Force 2783," I responded. "This is Wakkanai Dog Fox. Go ahead."

"Request bearing to your station. Over."

"Roger, stand by...bearing zero six eight. Got any mail? Over."

"Ah-roger, bearing zero six eight. Yes, two bags. Over."

"All-riiiight! Air Force 2783 this is Wakkanai Dog Fox. Your limo is waiting at the airstrip. See you. Over."

"Ah-roger. Air Force 2783 out."

The small, single-engine courier plane was a distant speck moving in over the low mountains before gradually assuming shape as it got closer. Air Force 2783 then circled the dirt and gravel airstrip and slowly bounced to a landing.

On board were the military pilot and one passenger, someone wearing civilian clothes who we later found was a special visitor from Washington.

Usually just an enlisted man or two and a Japanese guard met the infrequent courier planes but this time the site's Commanding Officer went with them.

They unloaded the mail sacks and some official bags from the plane to the jeep and posted the Japanese policeman to the first shift to guard the plane, an L-20.

Then the others crowded into the open jeep and drove back to the site.

Later, after the mail had been distributed and the civilian had been closeted with the Old Man, the pilot showered, ate, and dropped into The Barn, an old building that had been made into a combination recreation room, theatre and bar.

There he got to talking with a few of the off-duty enlisted men hanging around and playing ping-pong. The pilot, a second lieutenant, seemed to fit in right away. He was only 22 but still a little older than most of the others.

He had a pleasant and personable way about him and it later came out that he had been married for a year and was going to become a father within a few weeks. But he would not be able to see his new son or daughter for a year due to his overseas tour.

The pilot had not brought any extra clothing with him because he expected to be back at his air base the next day. So he showed up in the rec room in his flight suit.

The enlisted guys, dressed in fatigues, good-naturedly named him Space Cadet after a cartoon character of that name. It stuck.

The first night Space Cadet was at the site there wasn't much going on at the bar but he and a bunch of guys sat around telling stories, laughing and having a few beers. He was an officer and they were enlisted men but rank wasn't a factor. Just some new acquaintances sitting at a bar drinking socially in a far off land.

The next day Space Cadet wandered around the small radar detachment, chatting easily with those he met. It was a slow day for him as he waited for the civilian to finish his talks with the Commanding Officer.

The second night, still in his flight suit, he again dropped into The Barn, this time to watch one of the movies he had brought with the mail.

The movie was a two-year-old, three-reeler, and when the portable screen was put up on the ping-pong table and the lights turned off, the rec room became the theatre, with the informal atmosphere enhanced by the haphazard location of the chairs.

Each movie reel was shown in turn, rewound, and the next reel loaded and shown, resulting in two major intermissions. This allowed enough time to visit the latrine or get a fresh beer or coke at the bar.

There were pretty girls in some movie scenes and their appearance produced frequent yells from the audience of *"FOCUS!"* *"BACK-IT-UP!"* and *"SHOW THAT PART AGAIN!"*

When the film broke or got stuck and bubbled up with brown spots, boos and shouts of *"WHAT THE HELL DID YOU DO NOW?"* were directed at the volunteer projectionist, followed by multiple calls of *"LIGHTS!"*

It was noisy fun, and Space Cadet enjoyed it as he laughed at the comments and complaints. Afterward he and a few guys stopped at the bar in the next room for a beer before hitting the sack.

The third day was a repetition for Space Cadet, and he passed the time waiting for the civilian by playing ping-pong in the rec room and drinking coffee in the mess hall.

His personality and friendly manner drew guys naturally, and by now he had met almost everyone from the various night and day shifts. They liked him.

Early in the afternoon the civilian finally finished his business with the Old Man and Space Cadet and his passenger had to leave for another site down the coast, stay overnight, and return to Misawa the following day.

A few guys in a carryall followed the jeep to the dirt airstrip to see the courier plane leave and everyone was a little sad when Air Force 2783 took off.

They all watched as Space Cadet buzzed the site, wiggled his wings, and climbed into the clouds.

He'd be back.

~~~

...Radio operators rotated shifts at different radio jobs at the small radar site and my turn came up for a day shift at the main radio room the day after Space Cadet left.

It was a dull afternoon and I put my headset half on my ears and half on my temples. I leaned back in the chair and put my hands behind my head.

I looked out the window over the sandbags at the cloudy sky and thought that there could be some weather coming.

I listened to Morse Code on the frequency I was monitoring, and logged the infrequent transmissions.

Then I heard one of the other sites call Misawa with a priority message. I was bored and looking for something to do so I copied the encrypted text and decoded it.

It read:

Air Force 2783 crashed on takeoff this site x
no survivors x
request helicopter remove four bodies x

...I sat there. Stunned.

L-20 courier plane landing at Wakkanai International.

Twins

Paul's wife was due to have a baby and Paul was getting anxious and nervous.

He was a radar technician in the Air Force and stationed 9,000 miles away at a remote radar detachment in Northern Japan known as Site 18 while his wife was home in Indiana about to give birth to their first child.

At the small isolated radar detachment where Paul was, any personal messages such as births, deaths and family emergencies went through normal Red Cross and Air Force channels with the final leg of the message journey finished by Morse Code radio to the site. They were supposedly handled as quickly as possible all along the way.

When received in the site radio room the message was typed up and given to the Commanding Officer, who passed it on personally to the airman involved.

Those messages, usually with sad information, were rare but they did occur, and a system was in place on how to handle them.

Paul knew the personal message sequence long before the baby was due when he was told by a radioman how his message would get to him. But his anxiety took over his knowledge.

~~~

As time went on and Paul's wife was getting closer to the big day, Paul started asking any radio operators he ran into if his message had come in.

At first the radio ops went along with the question and said they would expedite the message through the Old Man when it came in, and Paul would know of its arrival within minutes.

At the small detachment of about sixty airmen and one officer everybody knew each other – no matter what their job was. So all the radio operators knew Paul, and since he was outgoing and friendly, they liked him.

As the date of the scheduled birth came closer and closer, Paul became more edgy and nervous. He was afraid he would not be notified right away when his message came in. He figured something would delay it in getting to him and he stepped up his questions to radiomen whenever he saw one.

Early on it had been kind of fun to answer him and to keep a lookout for his message but more and more it started to get on the nerves of some of the radiomen. They also wanted the message to arrive but for a different reason: they just wanted Paul to stop buggin' them.

Paul worked different shifts at the radar location on Hilltop a few miles from the site and when he was on duty there he started calling the radio room on the landline asking if his message had come in yet.

He made those calls once or twice on every shift he was on. And when he got back down on the site between shifts he started going to the radio room to ask in person.

No one was allowed in the radio room but the radio operators or maintenance men there to fix something, and Paul knew that. So he did not actually go into the radio room. He would just open the door, stick his head in, and ask whoever was on duty if his message had come in.

This seemed to go on for weeks, and started to wear on the radio operators. One in particular was getting sick of it. ...He also was a bit of a practical joker.

One day after Paul had called down from Hilltop twice and then went to the radio room door all within a few hours, that radio operator, not the most patient soul, had had enough. So he decided to end what he considered harassment by his friend.

The radioman got a blank message form, rolled it into the manual typewriter, and started typing.

When he was finished, he ripped it out of the typewriter, picked up the telephone, and called Paul's room, telling the guy who answered to tell Paul his message had come in. He said to tell Paul the message had to go to the Old Man but Paul could get a copy right now and to come to the radio room and get it.

Then he hung up the telephone and waited.

Within seconds heavy footsteps were heard running down the hall leading to the radio room and then the door burst open.

It was Paul. He did not go in; he just held the door open with one hand and stuck his head in yelling, *"Where's my message !! Gimme it !! Where is it ?!?"*

The radio op slowly took his headset off, placed it on the desk of the radio console, picked up the phony message and brought it over to the doorway where he handed it silently to Paul.

Paul took it, read it, and let out a whoop and a holler.

34

*"Its twins !! Its twins !! Its twins !! A boy and a girl !!
Everything is ok !! I'm a father of twins !! I'm a father of
twins !! Twins !! I'm a father !!"*

and Paul ran back down the hallway. He seemed to be
bouncing off the walls while yelling to everyone and to no one
in particular, *"I'm a father of twins !! A boy and a girl !!
Two of them !! Twins !! Yahooooo !! Twins !!"*

Other guys living or working in rooms off the hall came out
when they heard the yelling, and all smiled and gave congratula-
tions to Paul. It was a noisy and happy scene, and Paul handed
out cigars he brought with him after getting the phone call.

Meanwhile, the radioman down the hall watched from the
radio room doorway.

The excitement went on for some minutes, and as the radioman
watched he realized that his phony message and attempted practical
joke had brought more of a reaction from Paul than expected.

His intent was just to give Paul his 'message' and Paul would
go happily back to his room and probably write a letter home. Mail
would not go out for a week or so and the radioman figured that in
that time he would tell Paul the truth. Then Paul could retrieve his
letter before it left the site. Also during that time the real message
would probably arrive.

But Paul's extreme reaction and noisy celebration was so un-
expected that the radioman was sorry he had started the whole
thing with the phony message.

So he yelled down the hall to Paul and told him to come back,
which Paul did, holding out a cigar and wearing a big, expansive
grin and yelling, *"How about that - twins !!"*

35

Then on seeing the serious look on the radioman's face, Paul eyebrows became knitted in a quizzical look. He gave him a cigar and said, *"What's up?"*

The radioman said, *"It wasn't a real message. I made it up. I'm sorry. You've been buggin' me and other guys so much I thought I'd just type up a message to get you off my back. Your message hasn't come in yet. We'll let you know right away as soon as we get it."*

Paul was stunned. He just stood there and didn't say anything. Then he turned around and walked slowly back down the hall with head down and lips pressed together.

He was mad and he was sad. He was mad because he had been tricked into thinking he was the father of twins and he was sad because he had not received his message yet.

He wasn't mad at the radioman. Paul was a good sport. He knew no harm was meant and it was all a practical joke. So he shrugged it off. Nothing to stay mad about.

Meanwhile the radioman felt badly for awhile but in time he too forgot about it. It was the talk of the site for a day or two and then forgotten.

A few days later Paul's real message came in and he was told as soon as it arrived. It was a baby girl and mother and baby were doing fine. Paul was happy and relieved, and once again he passed out cigars to celebrate.

This time he was a little subdued. Paul's excitement had erupted so loudly and actively with the phony message that he was more under control when the real message came.

But he still had a huge expansive grin and happy eyes when passing out cigars. He was a father. For sure this time. Hontoh. A baby girl. Papa Paul.

~~~~~~~~~~~~~~~~~~~~~~~~~~~~~~~~~~~~~~~

Epilogue

The phony message was given to Paul in 1953 and in 1996, 43 years later, there was a reunion in Dayton, Ohio for the 511th AC&W, the parent organization of Site 18. About 20 guys from Site 18 were there as well as dozens from other sites.

This was the first big reunion and no one was sure who might attend. Expectancy and curiosity were in the air as most of us had not had any contact with each other for all those years.

Paul and I were among the attendees but I had not seen him as I walked into the crowded hospitality room with Al and Reno. Suddenly I heard a yell over the background noise of the dozens talking in the room:

"Hey, Waldron, was it you?"

Even though it had been 43 years since I had seen Paul I thought I recognized the voice. I looked around and saw him waving and yelling again, *"Over here; was it you?"*

He was over there talking with Big Red and Dick Loose and I went over, shook hands with each, and I said to Paul,

"What are you talking about?"

Paul said, *"The phony twins message when my daughter was*

37

born. I remember the message but I forget who typed it up. Was it you?"

"Oh ya. I remember that message too, but I dunno if it was me or not. That was a long time ago. Over forty years."

"It was either you or Ralph, and he's dead so we can't ask him. I think it was you anyway. Tell the truth. Was it you?"

"Maybe. I dunno. It cudda been me or, lemme think, it might have been Yo-Yo or Grover or Slim or Carlos or Bob or Tim or Al or John or Willie or Ted or Ralph or Dixie or Mel or even Red here. I forget. Cudda been anyone. There were lots of guys and lots of messages a long time ago."

"You're right. It was all kinda fun in a way, but I wish I could remember who typed the message and gave it to me."

"Yeah, me too. Who knows.   ...But anyway, Paul, tell me, how are the twins doin' these days?"

And we both laughed.

~~~~~~

Mohawk Haircuts

After lunch at the site I was bored and a little restless.

I had worked the midnight to eight shift in the main radio room and then slept the rest of the morning, and now I did not have to go back on shift until the next morning.

At lunch I heard that the old Japanese barber was on site for his monthly visit so I decided to get a haircut. When I got to the storage room where the barber was, he was standing there by a regular chair among the various supply boxes. There was no big mirror or any of the normal things seen in a barbershop.

No one was getting a haircut so I sat right down and the barber wrapped me in his small barber sheet.

It was at that point that the sudden thought occurred to me to get a Mohawk haircut.

I had no reason, other than why not? It just popped into my mind. I had been at the site for about a year and yet I still had 18 months before my 30-month tour would be up. If I got a Mohawk haircut for whatever reason, I figured my hair would grow back long before my time to go home.

So I told the old barber what I wanted. But there was a problem. He did not speak English, and my Japanese was terrible, especially since I had no idea what words to use to describe a Mohawk.

The barber had never heard the word Mohawk so that didn't do any good. As the old barber and I were not making any progress in trying to communicate about my request, Sal and Pooch, a couple of radar scope-dopes, came in for haircuts.

I told them I was trying to get a Mohawk haircut but the barber did not understand what I wanted and could they help. They immediately pitched in with gusto to help with hand motions and mixtures of English and Japanese.

Finally, the old barber at least partially understood, but his facial expression showed that he was leery of cutting it that way. He just wasn't sure what we meant and he did not want to cut it wrong and get into trouble.

But with the three of us talking and gesturing and laughing he finally understood and started using his electric clippers to get rid of most of my hair.

He stopped after the first run-through that made a path down to my scalp on the side to make sure this is what was wanted before continuing - although if it wasn't, it would have been too late.

When he was assured that that was just fine, he proceeded, with both Sal and Pooch talking and guiding him.

Before long all my hair was on the floor except for a two-inch wide short strip down the middle of my head that came to an arrow point in the rear.

When it was done, the three of us gave our approval to the smiling old barber, I paid him the two hundred yen – about fifty cents – and I said to Pooch and Sal, okay, who's next?

They looked at each other, arguing playfully that the other go first, all the while agreeing that what-the-hell, we're not goin' home 'til next year either so let's do it.

By now the old barber relaxed, understood what it was that we wanted, had learned a new American word, and knew how to cut a Mohawk haircut.

So this time he quickly gave Mohawk haircuts to Sal and Pooch. About the time the third one was done, Reno, from radio maintenance, walked in for a haircut.

He saw what was going on, saw how weird or unusual the three of us looked and how much fun we were having, so he figured, why not? me, too! And Reno joined Sal, Pooch and me and got a Mohawk.

The four of us went back to the day room where a couple of guys were playing ping-pong. We wanted to show off our new haircuts and see the reaction from whoever was there.

The guys in the day room liked what they saw, thought it was a neat idea and something to break up the monotony, and both went off to get Mohawk haircuts.

That afternoon a few more guys got Mohawks from the old barber and later almost all of us were in the mess hall at the same time for dinner, creating a buzz, double-takes, stares and pointed fingers.

A few more in the mess hall wanted to get Mohawks too, but it was too late as the old barber had gone home. Meanwhile the Japanese waitresses, Peggy, Aiko and Hedy, kept staring at us with quizzical looks. They couldn't figure out whether to laugh with us or at us as they giggled and rotated their index fingers near their ears in the well-known sign indicating someone was nuts.

One of the guys had manual hand clippers and after chow a bunch of us went up to the bar for a beer.

As we sipped our beer and chatted other guys drifted in. When they saw the clippers on the bar, some asked to join the group by getting a Mohawk too. So we obliged, using the manual clippers on them as they sat on a barstool.

A half dozen or so guys got Mohawks at the bar and as the evening wore on the noise and laughter grew.

Some had to have a few beers before they would take the plunge and volunteer. Others made it clear they wanted no part of it. Their lack of humor in response to our prompting convinced us to ignore them and leave them alone. It wasn't worth arguing.

But one guy in particular wanted no part of it but at least he did have a sense of humor. That was Al.

He didn't say why he didn't want a Mohawk but we all figured that it was because he liked his long wavy hair just the way it was, the hair that always looked like he had just combed it, which he probably had since he carried a small black comb and would take it out of his breast pocket and run it straight back, using both hands, on the top and along the sides to keep it neat. And to keep his hair from getting mussed up, he never wore a hat unless he was forced to by the weather or regulations.

Yes, Al's hair always looked so nice...

So it was not a surprise when he said *no way* was he going to get a Mohawk haircut. Not him. *No way*.

...Welllllll, there was a way.

It took five of us but we spread-eagled him on the floor with one guy sitting each leg and one guy sitting on each arm. The fifth guy had the clippers and sat on Al's chest.

Al was strong but the five were stronger and even he had to laugh at the helpless state in which he found himself.

The guy with the clippers sitting on Al's chest suggested that he not move around so much or struggle so much because the manual clippers would pull out clumps of hair which just might hurt a skoshe. Besides, it wouldn't look so pretty, now would it?

So the guy with the clippers strongly recommended that Al be still and allow the proceedings to proceed. And that meanwhile Al should shut up. But Al growled something about the Mafia and future revenge.

The suggestions were too late and Al's long, wavy, neatly trimmed hair came out in chunks. And he yelled in protest.

Regardless, he wouldn't be needing that comb in his pocket. But his hair looked so bad, what was left of it, and the fact that the stripe of a Mohawk could not be created, that we finally had to take all his hair off with the manual clippers.

Al was then bald, and looked like Mussolini.

At the end of the evening seventeen guys had Mohawk haircuts and Al was bald. There was a lot of hair on the floor.

There were only about sixty enlisted men and a couple of officers on site at the time and over 25% got Mohawks. There might have been more but they were either sleeping or working at the time and were not caught up in the fun.

We stayed that way for about three days and a lot of pictures were taken. Then Site 18 lapsed back to being as dull and as boring as it had been, at least for awhile – as if waiting for whatever might come next.

The Commanding Officer, Major Haines, wasn't too upset at what had gone on with the Mohawks although he did not come right out and endorse the event, at least directly. But a few days after what came to be known as the Massacre at Wakkanai, the major called me into his office.

He said he had been wondering who started the Mohawk thing but that it didn't really matter because no harm done and he said that now it was over. He didn't say why he had called only me into his office, and he wasn't too friendly as I stood in front of him, trying to keep a straight face.

He said the payroll officer was due to arrive from Misawa the next day and that I was to spread the word saying that everyone with Mohawks is hereby ordered to shave them off and to have bald heads before payroll.

He said Site 18 had a reputation at Misawa as having no discipline and that he did not want to add to the stories. So the word went out and we all shaved our heads, making us all as bald as cueballs, just like Reluctant Al.

When we reported for our pay the next day we went into the orderly room one by one, took off our fatigue hats exposing our shiny, bald heads, stood at attention, saluted smartly and recited our last name first, first name, rank to the payroll officer.

After he counted out the scrip and handed it to us, he had a quizzical look like we had seen from the un-massacred the last few days. He said nothing, and word spread through the site

grapevine, unconfirmed, that the payroll officer had been told
Site 18 had had a problem with head lice but it was under control.

The few days of the Wakkanai Massacre were now over. But
talk and smiles continued about the diversion, and the big mirror
in the latrine was a reminder for awhile.

It was fun while it lasted and, as was determined in the beginning,
all our hair grew back long before we went home – including Al's.

~~~~~~

Some Wakkanai Massacre survivors.
Front: Al Setting, Don Johnson
Middle: Paul Sheehan, Reno Giuntoli, Red Goodwin
Top: Cooler Everett, Bob Dietz, Sal Messina

Hey, youse guys, whaddaya think about the new barber?

To Teshio and Back

Cooler was a mechanic in the motor pool and was told at breakfast that he had to go to Teshio to fix a diesel power unit.

Cooler wasn't his real name; it was a nickname given to him because he was always smiling, snapping his fingers, and saying everything was cool, man.

Cooler asked Walt, a radio operator, can you get off from the radio room or swap with someone and go to Teshio with me, just to get away from the site for a day? we'd be back tomorrow.

Walt said maybe but I dunno. I just came down from Nob Hill but I don't have to go back up til tomorrow night. I'll check with Red.

Big Red, the DF radio NCOIC, said ok, you can go as long as you're back for your next shift on the hill.

Walt said sure no problem. See ya tomorrow.

Teshio was a small town on the west coast of Hokkaido, Japan. It was about a hundred miles from the Air Force radar detachment at Wakkanai, known to the Air Force as Site 18, where Cooler and Walt were stationed with about sixty other enlisted men and two officers.

Teshio's claim to fame from the Air Force point of view was that there was a two-man FM radio relay site on top of a small mountain whose purpose was to relay FM transmissions from

Site 18 on down to another relay site and then eventually to the main air base at Misawa, a few hundred miles south on Honshu.

Teshio's spare diesel power unit was on the blink and Cooler had to go fix it and bring spare parts, C-rations and mail for the two guys there. They were part of a rotation of radio maintenance men from Site 18 who spent a month at a time down there.

Walt would just be along for the ride with nothing to do other than help carry the supplies.

Jesse, a motor pool driver who was always a little drunk day or night, drove the six-by to the RTO train station, and on the way they stopped for four bottles of beer to take on the trip. Cooler and Walt rode in the back of the truck with a few boxes. They also had their carbines, a requirement while traveling to Teshio.

Jesse was always pleasant and smiling, which could have been from frequent sips of cheap whiskey, and everyone on the site liked him. So did the little kids along the mile-long dirt road between the site and downtown Wakkanai, a dirt-poor fishing village that seemed to be a hundred years behind the times. The kids knew Jesse by sight because he tossed out candy and gum to them as he drove past.

When they arrived at the RTO station Cooler laughed and complained to Jesse about the bumps and jolts and did Jesse hear the swearing coming from the back of the six-by? He said that Jesse should go back because he missed a pothole.

Walt chimed in saying to Jesse that they almost bounced out a couple of times and was Jesse aiming for all the potholes on purpose and why was Jesse mad at them?

Jesse laughed them off and told them not to give him a

*bad time like they always do. Besides, Jesse said, you
wouldn't want the Old Man to know that we stopped at
the store for some beer for your trip, would you? I
doubt if he would be happy knowing what else you had
in with those C-rations.*

*Cooler draped his arm around old Jesse, gave him a big
smile and told him he drove the safest and smoothest
six-by in all of Japan. In fact, Jesse should get a special
medal for being so capable. Scout's honor.*

*Jesse's smiling answer was unprintable as he helped the
two of them get their stuff off the six-by and onto the train.
Cooler told Jesse to mind the house while we're gone, and
not to worry too much because we shall return.*

Yeah, that's what I'm afraid of, said Jesse.

Bowing low, Walt added, syonara, Jesse-san, domo.

And so the travelers boarded the train while Jesse, with a wave,
headed the six-by back to the pot-holes and the site.

~~~

The locomotive was an old steam engine from long before WWII
and the passenger cars with their wooden seats seemed to be out of
an old cowboy movie. Teshio was about a hundred miles away but
because of many stops and delays the train trip would take almost
four hours. They wouldn't arrive until early afternoon.

Even though the Americans traveled first class coach a smell
was heavy in the air as they piled the C-ration boxes, mail pouch,
and parts boxes onto seats at one end of a passenger car. The end

50

seat faced the back of the train and the seat opposite faced to the front so the two faced each other with boxes on each seat.

They were dressed in fatigues and they propped their carbines against the wall under the window and put the ammunition clips in their pockets.

Once settled in their seats they really noticed the smell. It was body odor from the humidity mixed with the smell of seaweed, fish, and cooked noodles. Passengers had brought food on board and many ate with chopsticks while sitting in their train seats. Those eating used good manners, or so the GI's had been told, by loudly sucking the noodles into their mouths.

Cooler and Walt opened two of the bottles of beer they had bought on the way to the train station, and each lit up a cigar to distract them from the smells.

Cooler laughed and cussed at the unworking diesel generator at Teshio and Walt laughed and cussed at Cooler for asking him to go along for the trip. They then settled back, chatted aimlessly and stared out the window.

For the trip they had also picked up big meatloaf sandwiches from the mess hall, and around lunch time they ate them on the train with the other two bottles of beer.

When they finally got to the RTO at Teshio some hours later they were sober and no more rambunctious and happy than usual. The little beer they did drink just distracted them from the smell and sounds and heat on the train more than anything else.

~~~

The FM radio relay site at Teshio was on top of a very high hill, or small mountain. It was a few miles from the train station and arrangements had been made for Papasan to meet them with his horse and wagon and take them to the site since there were no military vehicles or taxis available.

Papasan was an energetic old man with a short, white beard and gold-filled teeth that showed conspicuously from his ever-present smile. He also nodded his head at everything that was said to him in English or in pigeon-G.I-Japanese, even if a word was not understood.

Despite the language and communication difficulties Papasan tried hard, and the guys who spent weeks at a time at Teshio liked him. He had been hired to bring visitors, supplies and food up the mountain and they used him and needed him.

On this day Papasan's wagon was not the one that Cooler had seen on a previous trip to Teshio. This was more like the chariots used by Roman gladiators in Coliseum races ages ago.

It was not as elaborate as a Roman chariot but the construction was similar. It had a waist-high railing around three sides and a small platform floor where the driver stood. There was no railing to the rear and no seats. The place for the driver was standing in the middle at the front holding the reins and a short whip.

Yep, it was a chariot alright. Of course it was.

Cooler and Walt looked at Papasan's wagon and said it sure did look like an old Roman chariot. Cooler said he thought that Roman gladiators might have looked a bit different in their bright and flashy outfits with bare legs and short skirts compared to the plain peasant clothes worn by Papasan and the drab, one-piece Air Force fatigues the Americans wore.

And the horse was not a snorting, pawing stallion. It was old, and had seen better days. Cooler went for a closer look to see if the horse was awake, and he told Walt he wasn't sure.

Then Cooler smiled and greeted the old man with the white beard, saying konichiwah, Papasan, ekaga-deska? - a polite way of saying hi, Pops, howzitgoin?

Papasan grinned from ear to ear showing all those shiny gold and white teeth and nodded vigorously while speaking rapidly in Japanese to the Americans who did not understand a word.

The three loaded the supplies on the chariot-wagon and then each made the high step and climbed on board. When they did so, the very old two-wheeled cart was crowded and creaked.

Hearing the noises and feeling the cart move, the old horse turned his sleepy head to the rear as if to say what's goin' on? When the horse looked back the movement caught Cooler's eye and he smiled at his sudden idea of naming the horse. So with a flourishing wave, he hereby dubbed it Nellie-san. ...What else?

Ya know, Walt seemed to be thinking out loud as he smiled as he looked at Cooler, does this remind you of a movie?   ...whaddaya think?
Hey that's cool, man, smiled the Cooler, and these here chances don't come along every day.

Using his pigeon-G.I.-Japanese, which was poor at best, and trying many hand-gestures and arm-waving, Walt asked Papasan if he could drive the chariot. Papasan didn't like the idea but Walt kept after him and Papasan reluctantly gave in.

After Papasan agreed, Walt took the reins and stood in the front middle of the platform, Papasan stood to the left holding on to the rail, and the Cooler stood on the right holding on to the other rail.

They were ready to roll.

They listened in vain for a blare of trumpets and a roar from the crowd as their imagined chariot race was about to begin. But the town was quiet and no one noticed.

Nellie-san neighed and snuffed, turned his head, gave another disgusted look back, and the harness jingled a bit.

In the Americans' eyes and vivid imaginations the old horse became a snorting stallion, the old cart became a gaudy chariot with saw blades sticking out of the spokes, the few Japanese watching silently became roaring spectators, and the dirt road near the RTO became the starting point to a chariot race at the Coliseum in Rome...

Of course it did.

Then with a loud EEE-HAW from Walt as he gave a stinging belt with the short whip on the rump of the 'stallion' the old nag lurched forward, faltered, lurched again, and off he went at a slow gallop up the dirt road as the few silent, passive onlookers moved out of the way.

Papasan held tight to the rail on the left with one hand, spoke excitedly in Japanese, and tried to get the reins back from Walt with his other hand. Meanwhile Cooler couldn't stop laughing as he held tight to the rail on the right side.

The town was very small and the chariot 'roared' through it, scattering a few chickens in the road and causing a dog to bark. A handful of curious faces turned to see what the noise was as Walt yelled and cracked the whip on Nellie-san's rump, and the horse responded with a slow gallop.

54

Shortly the quickly-tiring horse and the not-quite-Roman chariot was through and out of town.

It was all over within a noisy minute or so.

Walt still had the reins and didn't want to slow the horse down, but Nellie-san had enough. First he quit galloping and then he quit trotting. He went back to his preferred gait, walking slowly and so Walt handed the reins to Papasan.

After Papasan took the reins Cooler and Walt couldn't stop laughing. Papasan was mad at first but relaxed as he saw that his horse and rig had survived the short but explosive activity.

He also saw people in town, wide-eyed and smiling, wave as they returned the waves of the knee-slapping Americans as the noisy spectacle disrupted the serenity of the sleepy little hamlet.

Nellie-san had fared none the worse for his brief ordeal, and after Papasan let the horse rest a bit, the journey continued with Nellie-san pulling the chariot at his normal, slow, walking pace.

~~~

The cart creaked as they proceeded slowly on the dirt road, passing farms with men and women working in the fields who looked up and answered the Americans' waves.

The farmers working in the water-filled rice paddies wore bright colored shirts, pants rolled up to the knees, narrow head-bands with Japanese words marked on them, and kerchiefs.

They were both men and women, and some of the women had small children strapped on their backs in a sling.

In one field, two men worked alone and the backs of their light blue work shirts had the large letters 'PW' painted in black, a grim reminder of WWII that had ended eight years before.

The two ex-POW's were bent over and didn't notice the cart and three travelers until they had passed by. When they did see them, the two ex-POW's stood up and silently stared at the cart as it moved on down the road, looking passively at the two Americans with their carbines slung over their shoulders.

The trip to the bottom of the mountain took about an hour as neither Papasan nor the horse was in any rush. Cooler and Walt could have walked faster, and they did at times because standing and riding on the rig wasn't very comfortable. Like the train, the rig belonged to a distant past.

~~~

The road going up the mountain, which was more like a very steep hill, was too steep for the horse with the load plus the three passengers. So they stepped off the rig and walked, giving old Nellie-san just the weight of the cart and supplies to pull.

The winding road seemed about a mile to the top, and the dust and distance worked up a thirst among the travelers. Reno and Art were waiting for them at the top.

They had been there a couple of weeks and both had beards, grins and hearty hey howzitgoin'?

Cooler gave greetings from the outside world and asked what did they have for a drink. Even a coke would be good.

Art said never mind that; did you guys bring any mail?

Walt said that was no way to greet a tired visitor far from home, and yeah we have some mail for ya.

All of them unloaded the boxes from Site 18 and carried them into the radio shack.

Papasan got a coke and then went back out to take care of Nellie-san who snuffed and snorted as the old rig was unhitched. Papasan got the horse some water then sat down outside to rest. He was a little tired just like everyone else.

Before long, Papasan came into the shack, said he was leaving, and bowed. The Americans all thanked him, and Papasan went back out, hitched the wagon up, and started home, walking and leading his horse slowly down the mountain. Nellie-san followed with his head down, pulling the Roman chariot behind him.

~~~

The radio shack was a small two-room building built by the Japanese under contract to the Americans. It was fairly new and in pretty good shape.

One room had two bunks on opposite sides of the room, an oil stove, a table and a couple of chairs in the middle. The radio equipment was along the far wall opposite the door. The other room housed the two diesel power units.

Cooler and Walt were drinking a couple of cokes as Art and Reno sorted their mail by postmark and sprawled out on their bunks to read their letters in sequence.

It was chow time and while two read their mail the two visitors opened some C-rations, heated them on the oil stove, sat down at the table and ate.

57

The four talked idly about things on the mountain and back at Site 18, but Art and Reno were more interested in their mail. Chatter was light as two read and two ate.

After awhile Cooler asked about the diesel power unit that wasn't working, and then went to check it out.

He did not know how long it might take to fix, but as it turned out, he got it going within an hour. This was lucky because if a part was needed and not on hand it might take days or even weeks to get it.

With a big grin on his face Cooler came back, saying you guys called me all the way down here from the site to fix this thing? can't you do anything for yourself?

Art said to him, hey Reno and I are technicians, which means that we're not supposed to get our hands dirty.

Reno jumped in saying he had a story about Walt and how one night last winter when the snow was almost too deep for the weasel, Walt-san was up on Nob Hill and couldn't get any volume out of his DF equipment.

So, about two o'clock in the morning he calls the site on the landline and asks for a maintenance man to come up and fix it because we had a spy flight over Russia that night. I was on stand-by so I was elected. I woke up old Jesse, and we drove up to Nob Hill in the weasel in the middle of the night in a snowstorm. When we get up there, I fiddled and faddled and turned up the volume knob and it worked perfectly. For that I lost a night's sleep.

Wait a minute yelled Walt. Not so. Whatever you did

58

was inside the receiver, not the outside knob. There's
a big difference!

Reno, laughing, said the fact remains, O'Marconi,
that I had to go out in the middle of the night in the
middle of a blizzard and half freeze to death and
almost get killed on that winding road to Nob Hill
just to turn up your volume.   ...Even Walt had to
laugh at the memory.

~~~

Since Cooler had been able to get the diesel power unit back on-line, the job was done and he and Walt had to think about getting back to Wakkanai. The next train was in mid-morning so they had to stay overnight somewhere, and there wasn't enough room in the radio shack.

So after sitting around for awhile with Art and Reno, talking about everything and nothing, they decided to go back into town, get a room and catch the morning train.

~~~

Cooler and Walt walked down the mountain road as the sun was setting. They looked out over the Sea of Japan toward Far East Russia that they thought was Siberia, and they knew that over there out of sight to the left was the war in Korea.

Streaks of red reached into the sky from the dull red sun as it slowly disappeared below the horizon. All was peaceful and quiet as the two walked down the mountain watching the sunset colors fade away.

It didn't take too long to get to the bottom and then Cooler and

Walt continued along the road leading into town. They hoped to catch a ride with a farmer going into Teshio in a wagon.

After walking on the dusty road awhile and seeing no signs of life other than farmers still working in the fields, they came to some railroad tracks heading toward town. Figuring the tracks were more direct and would save some time they decided to walk them.

Not long after, as they walked the tracks a hundred yards from the road they heard the sound of a vehicle. It was too far away to get it to stop so they just swore at their luck and watched to see what it was. Around a bend in the road with a following cloud of dust came what looked like a brand new red 1953 Plymouth hardtop.

Walt and Cooler stood there staring dumbfounded with jaws hanging open. They were speechless. It was so out of place.

First of all, there were very few cars on Hokkaido and those few were old.

Second, Teshio was a small town in the mountains with dirt roads for miles. A car like that might be found in a big city, like Tokyo a thousand miles south, not Teshio.

Third, the car looked like a new one and it might have been American but they couldn't tell. They had not seen any 1952's or 1953's except maybe in an ad in a magazine, so the two of them were amazed.

It was weird, and completely out of place. Then the red car was gone, with a dust cloud settling in its wake. A bit downcast, Cooler and Walt continued walking the tracks and wondered out loud if they both had seen what they both saw.

~~~

But their luck changed.

Coming toward them along the single train track from Teshio
was a railroad handcar propelled by a trainworker sitting on a
bicycle seat and peddling along the track like a bicycle.

The handcar had a bicycle seat on each side, an open platform
in the middle, a railing in front, and was about five feet long.

The two Americans in their fatigues with carbines on their backs,
waved down the man in the handcar and as it slowed to a stop they
saw a big 'combat jug' of saki hanging from the front railing.

The trainworker smiled and appeared happy and friendly but
he did not speak any English. In their best attempts at speaking
G.I./Japanese, Cooler and Walt, with hand, arm and body signals,
asked him if he would turn the handcar around and give them a
ride to the RTO station a few miles away.

He was willing, and after hiding the combat jug of saki in the
weeds and marking the spot with a white rag, the three of them
lifted the handcar off the tracks, turned it around, and set it back
on the tracks heading to Teshio.

Of course Walt and Cooler wanted to do the peddling and the
man shrugged and agreed. So he took a position in the middle
holding on to their shoulders and Walt and Cooler got on the
bicycle seats on each side. They grabbed the handle-bars, and
off they went peddling down the railroad tracks toward town.

It was hard to say who enjoyed the trip more, the G.I.'s or
the trainworker. Cooler and Walt peddled furiously to get up
some speed and then the whole scene struck them funny. They
started laughing and couldn't stop, and the railroad man joined
in as Walt and Cooler peddled and peddled.

The track was not straight and curved around a few farms and hills, with some upgrades and downgrades. On the downgrades they were clipping along over the tracks with good speed, huffing, puffing and enjoying themselves.

They yelled and laughed and peddled the whole time and when they reached Teshio they were weak from it all. Then the three picked up the handcar, turned it around, and set it back on the tracks in the other direction.

They started to give the smiling trackworker two hundred yen, about fifty cents American, but he refused even though it might have been a day's pay to him.

With friendly waves from each, the trainman got on a bicycle seat and started peddling back along the tracks, hoping he would be able to find the white cloth that marked his hidden jug of saki as it was getting dark. He would chuckle later telling his family a story about two Americans he had met today.

~~~

Teshio was a small town with one main street a few blocks long with some short side streets branching off, all unpaved. The buildings were wood and one story high and the main street had small shops. It was a remote, poor village that seemed far removed from the modern 1950's and the twentieth century.

They found the one tea shop and went in, intending to ask the location of the rooming house that Reno and Art told them about.

The tea shop was small, one-room, dimly lit and reeked of fish. Two old men sat silently at a table smoking long-stem pipes, with small cups of warm saki before them.

62

It was getting dark and Walt and Cooler were tired. But instead of getting a beer and sitting down for awhile in the tea house, the smell of fish got to them. So they bought a small bottle of saki and went back out to the street to look for a place to spend the night.

The town was almost deserted as they looked for the rooming house where the tea shop owner had indicated, and they finally found it. It seemed to be owned by an old couple and Cooler and Walt got two small rooms for the equivalent of a dollar each.

There was no dining room but when they said they were hungry the old man and woman went to their kitchen and fixed a meal of rice, eggs and tea for them.

The four then sat on the floor in the 'lobby' around a charcoal hibachi pot, while the Americans tried with difficulty to eat with chopsticks. Mamasan and Papasan knew no English so they tried to use Japanese words that the Americans knew. The attempts to communicate were humorous but the efforts made the meal very pleasant and friendly.

After the meal Mamasan and Papasan heated the saki the G.I.'s had with them and the four continued sitting on the floor, the two Americans sitting cross-legged and the two Japanese sitting on their heels. Everyone tried to talk slowly and with limited vocabulary as best they could about Japan and America.

As there were no beds Cooler and Walt slept on bamboo mats rolled out on the floor of their tiny rooms, and had heavy quilts for blankets. They left their boots in the hallway and in the morning, after leaving an extra 100 yen in each of their rooms as a tip, they ate breakfast of rice, eggs and tea Mamasan made for them, put their boots on, thanked the older couple for everything, paid for the rooms and meals, and walked down to the RTO to catch the train.

~~~~

At the RTO, as the old steam locomotive dragged the train slowly into the old station, Cooler asked Walt if he had brought any extra cigarettes.

Walt had two unopened packs and asked why, since he knew Cooler didn't smoke cigarettes.

Cooler explained that ever since he was a little kid in Indiana he had wanted to ride up in the engine of a train with the engineer and blow the train whistle.

He said maybe we could ask the engineer if we could ride up there in the cab with them and maybe we could bribe him with a pack of cigarettes.

Walt said why not try it, we have nothing to lose.

The two fatigue-wearing, carbine-carrying, unshaven G.I's walked up to the locomotive and tried to explain their offer and request to the train engineer who was leaning out the window watching the few passengers get on board.

The Americans had a hard time explaining what they wanted to do but the engineer finally understood and he laughed, saying they were like little boys. When the engineer smilingly consented, Cooler and Walt, with grins and some effort, climbed up into the cab of the old coal-burning steam engine.

~~~

They stayed out of the way and watched while the fireman shoveled coal into the boiler and the engineer adjusted a dial or two. Then the engineer leaned out the window, looked back along the platform, pulled a cord over his head, and with a steam train whistle sound the engine chugged slowly and got underway.

Once out of the station and into the countryside the G.I.'s looked around and asked about the various controls and gadgets in the cab. The questions and answers involved body language and gestures because the engineer and fireman, although friendly and cooperative did not speak English while Walt and Cooler spoke only G.I.-Japanese.

As the old steam train continued along the trainmen got caught up in the scene and were enjoying it. This probably did not happen every day to them either...

Cooler sat at an open side window and said to Walt that this was one crazy iron horse.

Walt pointed to a metal nameplate on the console and said look at this, the engine was Made In England! There's no date but it had to be years before WWII.

Cooler asked the engineer if he could pull the train whistle cord, and made a whistle sound as he asked and pointed to the cord and then himself.

The older engineer, who they naturally called Papasan, smiled and pointed to the two cords, one on each side of the cab, then he pointed to Walt and Cooler, and nodded his head. That started it.

Cooler sat at one side of the cab at the window and Walt sat on the other side at the opposite window.

Walt was a radio operator and after Cooler pulled the cord to make long train whistle sounds, Walt tried to send Morse Code with his train whistle but couldn't do it.

Both smiled and waved to farmers working in their fields and they blew the whistles over and over as the old train chugged through the countryside. Passengers on the train must have thought that strange goings-on were happening up front at the locomotive, and farmers in the fields may have felt the same way.

Walt and Cooler, sober in the morning air, were enjoying a fun ride they would not soon forget. They shoveled coal, watched the dials, pulled the cords, waved at the farmers, talked in Japanese and English, and thoroughly enjoyed their ride through the rural countryside.

After awhile everything settled down and the novelty wore off. The day was beautiful and their curiosity had been satisfied.

But they did not like the idea of leaving the fresh air in the open cab of the old steam engine and going back to riding in a hot and smelly passenger car.

At one of the many stops, they got off to stretch their legs and Walt said that he had an idea as he looked back along the train at the three passenger cars and a few freight cars.

Cooler was game so he asked what was the idea?

Walt told him look way down to the back of the train and see those couple of empty and low coal cars; so, whaddaya think?

Cooler said why not?

They thanked the engineer and fireman, gave them the two packs of cigarettes, answered their bows with their own slight bows, and trotted down the station platform to the end of the train to the empty coal cars.

On the way they saw a couple of small wooden crates and took them with them for seats in case the inside of the car was dirty. They threw the crates into the low open coal car, climbed in, propped up the crates in opposite corners at the rear, and sat down. They were in the last car of the train and out in the open.

The air was fresh, the breeze welcome, the train did not go very fast, and the scenery was pleasant.

Cooler and Walt quieted down and lit up cigars as they sat on the crates, each in a back corner of the coal car. Their arms were stretched out on top of the car's walls as they relaxed and enjoyed the ride, just looking out at the hills and farms.

Their only problem came when the train went through a couple of short tunnels and the smoke from the chugging coal locomotive enveloped them for a few seconds. But they still preferred the open coal car to riding in a crowded and smelly passenger car.

At a train stop they saw a sign listing the train schedule and saw that Wakkanai was next. So they decided to leave the open coal car and ride the last few miles inside a passenger car in case anyone from the site was at the RTO with their friend Jesse.

They knew that the Old Man had to go into town now and then and therefore could be with Jesse. If so, they doubted that the Old Man would appreciate seeing them climb out of an open coal car at the back of the train.

But it was only Jesse at the RTO to meet them, and they asked if he had missed them.

He hadn't, and he asked if everything was okay in Teshio and did they have a good trip.

Cooler told him that all was fine in Teshio and the trip was cool, man. Just plain vanilla. Still smiling, Cooler snapped his fingers.

~~~

67

This time, with no packages and boxes and just their carbines, they climbed in front of the six-by with Jesse as he drove back to the site, bouncing the three of them all the way as he hit many potholes and ruts in the dirt road. The two were convinced that Jesse never tried to avoid a pothole. ...Maybe he didn't see them

They got back to the site in time to take a shower and get to the evening chow. After eating with Dixie and Slim and telling them some of the things about their trip, Walt and Cooler had to go different ways.

Walt rode the weasel on the two mile, uphill, bumpy, winding ride to his overnight DF shift on Nob Hill. No shift time had been lost, but Big Red had been asking if anyone had seen Walt because Walt had better be back for the next shift at Nob Hill and why wasn't he back yet from Teshio. Red was a bit edgy, but no sweat, Walt had made it in time.

As for Cooler, after chow he headed to the bar for a beer and to tell stories about the trip.

As he walked out to the renovated barn
where the bar was, Cooler ran into Tim.

Tim said, hey man, how'd it go at Teshio?

Cooler smiled and said, fine, man. everything's cool.

And he snapped his fingers with a big grin on his
face as he bopped along the path to the barn.

Epilogue

This little story is true and is dedicated to the memory of Merle Everett, better known as The Cooler.

~~~

Some months after this Teshio trip Cooler was injured seriously in an accident at Site 18.

It was his back that was injured, and he traveled south to see Air Force doctors who told him that a minor operation should fix up his back just fine.

So he had the minor operation.

But a mistake was made on the operating table and his spinal cord was cut, making Cooler a quadriplegic for the rest of his life, which turned out to be about forty years.

Some guys from Site 18 saw Cooler a few times back home in Indianapolis before he died and they said that he kept his smile and upbeat attitude from his special wheelchair more than they had expected.

But one time he did say, with a smile as always, that the worst thing about being a quadriplegic was that he couldn't even commit suicide, man.

He said that while drinking a beer through a straw, and he probably would have snapped his fingers if he could have.

~~~~~~

The Cooler

Sapporo and the
Army Lieutenant

In the summer of 1953 Captain Larry Charbonneau, Commanding Officer of Site 18 at Wakkanai, got on the landline with Misawa and some other site C.O.'s and they put together a baseball tournament among the sites to be played at the Army base in Sapporo.

Not all sites could attend because either they did not have enough baseball players or not enough players could be spared from their jobs because of a lack of replacements.

But there were a few sites that sent teams, and we had a fun baseball tournament for a few days at the very big Army base in Sapporo, which was the home of the Army's First Cavalry Division at the time.

The tournament was won by Misawa — not surprising given the number of people they had available compared to the small number of personnel at each site. But still it was fun.

About the only thing I remember about the trip was the time some of us 'got in trouble' and were chewed out by an Army second lieutenant while we walked to the PX.

A few of us were in our fatigues and probably not looking very military-like, and we failed to salute some passing Army second lieutenants as we walked along talking among ourselves. We may not have noticed the lieutenants. But more probably we were not used to saluting officers in passing since we had spent many months on a small site where informality ruled and there were only one or two officers on the premises.

After we had passed by them, one young second lieutenant yelled at us and told us to halt right there.

We stopped, turned, and wondered what this guy's problem was as he walked aggressively back to us, squint-eyed and growling with his hands on his hips. It was a scene from a B-movie.

He then called us to attention and started chewing us out, demanding to know who we were and why we were out of uniform and why didn't we snap off a salute to him and his fellow officers as they walked by in the opposite direction. He had a whole bunch of screaming questions. We stood there at attention wondering just what was going on and who the hell was this idiot.

But he might have had a point. We probably had white socks on, no hats or non-military baseball hats, no stripes on our fatigues, open buttons, and no doubt presented a what-the-hell attitude as we strolled along chatting.

So we told the second lieutenant who we were, reciting some-thing like: Sir. Air Force, from a radar detachment up north at Wakkanai, part of the 511th Aircraft Control and Warning Group based in Misawa, sir, at a baseball tournament here, sir.

Despite our reply of facts he continued to be flustered as he yelled more about our appearance and apparent attitude. And, well, maybe it was a good thing he could not read our minds as we stood there at attention, each thinking of a word describing him that begins with the letter 'a' - make that a capital 'A'.

Unsaid were thoughts of yessir, nossir, three-bags-full-sir, and other mocking words unfit for the home dinner table. What we did say were facts that went over his head as meaningless, and it showed by the confused and quizzical look on his face.

The second lieutenant then promised to contact our Commanding Officer to tell him what a disgrace we were, what poor examples of the United States Air Force we were, and, of course, we should realize we were in big trouble.

We stood there wondering just what is it with this guy?

He finally let us go after duly impressing his fellow smirking second lieutenants who watched silently as the little charade played out. He may have been right, but our straight-faces and silent demeanor concealed our attitude which was, ok, whatever you say, can we go now?

For some reason the second lieutenant did follow up with his threat and did leave a complaining message with Captain Charbonneau who was in charge of the tournament, and he called us aside.

He asked if what he had been told about the street encounter with an Army second lieutenant was true, and we said it was.

And the captain, who started as an enlisted man in the Army in WWII, became an officer and P-47 fighter pilot with 99 combat missions on D-Day and later, and also served as a forward tank observer on the ground with Patton's army, smiled as he told us to behave. He said he knew a little bit about the Army, and that we should not forget that we are guests here. This was their Army base and they're used to doing things different from what we're used to back at the site.

Then he chuckled as he said we should concentrate on more important things like winning tomorrow's baseball game.

~~~~~~

Site 18 baseball team - Sapporo site tournament in 1953. (back row): Dick Waldron, Bob Benning, John Nauman, Paul Sheehan, Ed Dube, Gordon Locklear, Bob Mueller, (front row): Al Setting, Frank Ciarniello, Bob Cole, Captain Charbonneau (Site 18 C.O.)

Inspection on Horseback

It was the summer of 1953 and never before had there been a scene at Site 18, an Air Force radar detachment, and probably nowhere else, of

> *an open ranks inspection*
> *in Class A uniforms,*
> *carrying dusty carbines,*
> *wearing soft-brimmed cowboy hats,*
> *with the inspecting officers on horseback.*

I say again: 1) Air Force troops in cowboy hats.
                2) officers on horseback.

But it happened. And it came as a complete surprise because there had not been any kind of formal inspection during the few years the site had existed.

I like to think Major Haines, Site 18's Commanding Officer, had received word from Misawa headquarters suggesting that he have an inspection before he rotated home.

And I like to think that he mentioned the suggestion to Captain Charbonneau, the incoming C.O., as well as telling a few enlisted men at the bar.

And I like to think an enlisted man told them that it was ok to have an inspection as long as we could do it our way.

That is what I would like to think. But in reality, I can't find any-one who remembers who's idea it was and exactly how it all began.

The captain later said he was in on it early on and that he was later blamed at headquarters for the episode. He said that his boss, a colonel at Misawa Air Base, showed disapproval by "reflecting as much in my Efficiency Report."

But Captain Charbonneau added in a letter that he was glad it had happened and that he enjoyed the event. He wrote, "It made everyone happy and morale went through the roof that day."

Frank Watanabe, the Japanese interpreter wrote about his role in the inspection saying that the Captain asked him to do two things. Frank wrote:

" (1) In regard to the horses: It was a little before the fourth of July and Captain Charbonneau came to me and asked that I get two horses from downtown without saying why he needed them.

I went to see my friend who owned the horses to ask if he would let us use them one day on the site. He gave me the ok.

I told Captain Charbonneau that I could get the horses and that I needed two bottles of CC right away.

The next day the owner came to the site with the two horses for Major Haines and Captain Charbonneau to practice with for a couple of hours.

The day of the inspection the owner brought the horses to the site and stayed to make sure everything went well.

The horses those days were pretty important for transportation during the winter for Japanese employees to come to work on the site and get back home. During the summer the horses pulled wagons hauling coal for the boiler plant on the site.

(2) The hats: Captain Charbonneau showed me a picture of a cowboy hat and said he wanted the same type of hat.

I told him that it was impossible to get from town. But anyway, I went to Takabayashi clothing store and asked the owner to get me similar type. He gave me a sample of a hat and I showed it to Captain Charbonneau. He ok'd it. A week later the store owner got the hats from Sapporo."

While this was going on, few if any enlisted men knew what was planned. Maybe a couple who did know were asked to keep it quiet.

The notice of the upcoming inspection was posted on the bulletin boards outside the mess hall and outside the orderly room. The notice stated that there would be an open ranks inspection in Class A uniforms with carbines at nine o'clock on such-and-such a date for all personnel not on duty or had not worked the night before. And everyone was to go to the orderly room to get a hat.

... A hat???   What's that all about???

The guys were not too happy. There had never been an inspection of any kind, except occasionally the C.O. might walk into a room, look around, say this should be straightened out or that should be cleaned up, and leave. But that's all.

Naturally, the guys complained and muttered to themselves.

... What's goin' on? ... What's happ'nin'? ... Do you know? What's this about hats? ... Why don't they leave everything alone? ... We don't want any kind of open-ranks blankety-blank inspection ... Who needs that nonsense? ... How can I get out of it? ... Hey, what's with the hats? ... Never mind that, what's with the carbines? ... I dunno, all's I know is mine's covered with dust ... Doesn't matter to me, I'm working ... Lucky you.

The soft-brimmed civilian hats were the closest to be found similar to the cowboy hats requested, and were to add flavor to the open ranks inspection with horses.

But the troops didn't know about the horses either.

The hats and horses were obtained by Frank, the interpreter, and he just shrugged when asked about the boxes of hats in the orderly room. Nobody knew about the horses so Frank wasn't asked about them.

In my case, Al and I had worked the midnight-to-eight shift and were allowed to skip the inspection. We figured we were lucky we didn't have to go play soldier that morning.

But we missed out, not witnessing anything except watching roommates Slim and Grover and Yo-Yo reluctantly walk outside and stand around with the others before the inspection. Al and I looked out the window then hit the sack and slept the rest of the morning, glad we were excused. ...Later we wished we weren't.

From laughing descriptions given and from the photographs, about twenty-five enlisted men in fell out for the inspection that summer morning.

They wore Class A summer uniforms with crushed, folded, soft-brimmed 'cowboy' hats, carried carbines, and grumbled as they assembled in the open area in front of the motor pool. The hat brims and tops were bent and creased this way and that so the appearance of the troops was not consistent.

They milled around and relaxed in the morning sun, joking about the scene and saying how weird it was to put on a dress uniform at the site, a uniform some had not worn for a couple of years.

Buck, the first sergeant, told them to form three ranks, then called them to attention. He had them dress right dress, and then gave the command to rest.

With the formation at rest, all eyes were attracted to sounds and sights at the front gate where Arlie and Reno were coming toward them with two horses.

Horses ???

Arlie was walking ahead leading one horse by the reins and Reno was riding a horse behind him.

What's that all about ? ... What's with the horses ? ... What's going on ? ... Did you know anything about this ? ... Not me ! ... Do you see that ? ... What-the-helllll ???

They saw Major Haines, standing by the motor pool door, light up a cigar with Captain Charbonneau next to him, and both were grinning from ear to ear. The troops, standing loosely in formation, saw the relaxed officers and their two friends with horses, and figured this blankety-blank inspection might not be too bad after all.

The horses were brought to the major and the captain and the two officers climbed up into the saddles.

The major, being a skoshe overweight and out of shape, needed some help to get himself up there but he made it. He had a cigar clamped between his teeth, wore a soft-brimmed hat like everyone else, and just beamed as he sat in the saddle smiling down at the guys before him.

The captain, also wearing the hat of the day, was smiling too and seemed more at ease on his horse than the Major as

80

they sat on their horses side by side before the troops.

Meanwhile the guys were laughing and commenting, or just staring open-mouthed at the scene.

The major called the formation to attention and gave the command to dress right, dress. After some shuffling and alignment, the troops finished and the major called out: two; at ease. The troops dropped their arms and stood at ease.

Both the major and the captain smiled, and the major said something like now, that wasn't too bad. I'd say it needs some work though. He grinned sitting there on a horse while chewing a cigar and looking over the troops.

Then the captain dismounted and handed the reins to Arlie, while the major stayed on his horse. The captain told the first sergeant to call the troops to attention and to go to port arms.

Buck did as ordered, and he and the captain proceeded to walk down each rank, stopping at each man standing at port arms, and each wearing a non-government-issue civilian hat.

At each man the captain stopped, looked at the man's uniform, made some comments, took the man's carbine, inspected it, handed it back to the man, and went on to the next man. The first sergeant followed behind him and the major sat up on his horse watching.

When the individual inspections were completed, the troops were called to attention, and then dismissed. It had taken less than an hour and now it was done.

The guys smiled, chatted and slowly dispersed as the major dismounted and handed the reins to Reno. They had completed their inspection, and Misawa headquarters would be informed, with perhaps an unnecessary detail or two left out of the report.

But there was an exclamation point on it among the guys as an inspection to remember. You know, the one that caused smiles when reminded decades later.

Because, no one could forget the time there was an open ranks inspection at Site 18 with the officers on horseback and everyone was in Class A uniforms with carbines and 'cowboy hats'.

If there were a vote, I'm sure all would agree with Captain Charbonneau's assessment when he wrote fifty years later,

"It made everyone happy and morale went through the roof that day."

I didn't realize it then but this added a bit to the maverick reputation Site 18 apparently had among other sites and head-quarters. This was brought to my attention months later in Misawa when I was asked about life at Site 18 because, as I was told, everyone knows things happen at Site 18 that did not happen at other sites and that Site 18 is something else.

... I dunno about that ... what things? ... then again, well, maybe ... who knows ... not me, I don't know nuthin' ... so, tell me, what have you heard?

Capt. Charbonneau on left, Major Haines on right. aka: Tonto on Scout and the Lone Ranger on Silver.

Haines' Rangers in their Sunday best.
(far left): John Nauman; (facing camera): Gene Buckley (1st Sgt); Sandy Friedman, Red Rife, Slim Peninger, Grover Ashcraft

Paul Markovich (second from left),
not the father of twins, and either a few commands
ahead of everyone else or a few commands behind.

Ham Radio

Site 18 had a ham radio station with the most powerful ham radio signal in the world.   …I say again: the most powerful ham radio signal in the world.

'Course, that's not to say it was the most legal ham radio signal in the world. That's a different subject.

In 1953 the new MARS station (aka ham station) had a signal beaming back to the States with 2000 watts of power at a time when the FCC limit for Stateside hams was 1000 watts.

Our signal was twice the allowable limit but since there was a question of FCC jurisdiction and enforcement, and the potential military use through the MARS system (Military Auxiliary Radio System), those that put the station together goosed up the power.

There were no other MARS stations on Hokkaido nor were there any known Japanese ham stations. We had the big island to ourselves as far as MARS was concerned, and were surprised to learn that the Army's First Cavalry Division on Hokkaido did not have one. Nor did any other Air Force radar site at the time. The closest MARS station was hundreds of miles away on Honshu at Misawa.

~~~

The very strong radio signal of the MARS station at Site 18 was because of the unusual and huge antenna and a modified transmitter.

The antenna was a rhombic configuration stretched among three very high poles which were more than twice as high as a typical telephone pole. The antenna was therefore fixed in place as opposed

86

to the typical movable ham antenna called a rotary, as in '20-meter band rotary antenna.' The rhombic was aimed out over the ocean toward the United States.

The transmitter used at Site 18 was a modified BC-610 , the common military ground transmitter with a rated power output of about 400 watts. Rewiring and modifying it for MARS use resulted in a power output of 2000 watts.

It rocked.

At the time that the FCC allowed a maximum power output of 1000 watts most American hams had 200-to-300 watt transmitters or less, and hams in other countries used even smaller power.

~~~

Trivia: Hams and MARS stations used both voice and CW transmission. The term CW comes from Continuous Wave, a type of signal that when transmitted is broken into the Morse Code dits and dahs.

~~~

Major Haines, the Commanding Officer of Site 18, and Flip Claunch, a civilian Philco tech rep, were both licensed hams when they decided to build a MARS station on the site.

Flip handled the technical stuff, a 10' x 10' unused guard shack was commandeered, a few guys helped with carpentry to build a console, and the major handled all the paperwork by mail with the FCC in Washington. The major also took care of recruiting of radio operators needed to get FCC licenses. ...I was one of three that he volunteered.

All of the above took a couple of months to come together under their direction and drive. The rest of us knew nothing about ham radio and were more curious than excited about what was going on.

After the new station was completed it took time for us new guys to learn ham language and customs. For instance, we had to send and receive Morse Code extemporaneously – much easier said than done after our strict message construction with Air Force CW messages.

The same goes for voice communications where we suffered 'mike fright' when trying to learn to speak off the cuff and not in the clipped and specific Air Force voice method. There were even new phonetic letters hams used that differed from military ones. But we learned. I later heard of hams who would use only voice or only CW, but not both because they were uncomfortable with one.

~~~

When all was completed and the new MARS rig was on the air, the station was open at any time to those who had a ham license. But our availability was limited to time off between regular radio shifts which varied daily with shift rotations.

Once the word got out that calls home via the radio using something called a phone patch, a lot of guys were interested.

But three limitations remained: operator availability, weak incoming signals, and competition from other MARS stations in Korea, Okinawa, Iwo Jima, Guam and southern Japan. All were fighting to get through to the few Stateside hams with phone patch equipment and the willingness to put through calls because of the extra time necessary.

So it wasn't a case of deciding to call home, walking out to the ham shack, and calling home. Guys might wait days to make a phone patch or sit in the radio shack for hours as attempts were made. But the frustration was worth it when calls got through and a guy talked to someone at home on the other side of the world.

The way phone patches worked was first to hook up with a ham with a strong signal and phone patch equipment, tell him a number to be called, and who was calling. The ham, anywhere in the country, would place a collect telephone call from his home on behalf of the caller, telling the operator he had a collect call from so-and-so.

The long distance operator would place the call, ask if they would accept a collect call from so-and-so (a stranger, the ham, in Chicago or anywhere). Sometimes the person answering declined to accept the charges, especially if their phone rang in the middle of the night, saying their son or husband wasn't in Chicago, he was in Japan.

Once the collect call was accepted, the ham placed his telephone in his phone patch cradle and he and the MARS operator stood-by to switch their equipment back and forth between transmitting and receiving as the two parties alternated speaking and listening.

The conversation was a bit stilted and awkward because talking on a phone patch was not like talking on a telephone. With a phone patch, one person could not talk when the other was talking. They had to take turns, speak a few sentences, stop, say 'over', then have the other party speak. It could be an unnatural conversation. At each change the two hams would switch from transmit to receive or from receive to transmit.

It also could be a little self-conscious for a guy to be talking to his wife or girl friend with a MARS operator sitting there and a ham in the States having to listen so each would know when to switch from transmit to receive, and back. But we hams were interested in the signal strength and clarity rather than the conversation.

The people answering the phone at home did not know how it worked and sometimes it took two or three explanations to have both sides understand that one spoke and one waited and each had to speak, then wait, then speak, then wait. If they said 'over' or if the conversation was at an obvious pause then the ham operators

89

would switch their rigs from transmit to receive, or back.

Altogether it was sometimes time-consuming and somewhat awkward but in the end the effort was worth it, especially to hear the excitement of the voices on both ends of a phone patch.

~~~~

Radiograms were also sent through the MARS station. These were sent by CW to hams in the States who copied down the incoming messages, typed them on Western Union-type message forms, typed the address on an envelope, added a stamp and mailed them. Some hams copied messages for hours at a time then spent more hours typing them up for mailing – all without any pay of any kind. It was their hobby and they did it to help G.I.'s overseas.

(Later when I worked in the big MARS station in Misawa I dealt regularly with a ham in Seattle named Leo with a call-sign W7IOQ, as in, as he said, I Oughtta Quit. We received many radiograms by teletype from a couple of locations in Korea and relayed them to the States, mostly with Leo. I sent them with an electronic speed key, he taped them, and the next day he would type the messages and mail them. Sometimes I sent him 10 messages in a row, asked if he got them ok, got a quick 'r' from him, and kept going. It was fast and efficient.)

Radiograms used shortcuts with a three-number code system for standard greetings selected from a ham handbook. This allowed faster transmission and less errors since numbers were easier to copy than longer words. The receiving ham later translated the code number into the greeting phrase when he typed the message to mail.

~~~~

The call-sign at Site 18 was K-A-9-W-H, and like many hams, we made the call-sign into our own phonetic alphabet phrase that was easy for other hams to recognize. Just as Leo, W7IOQ, used 'this is I Oughtta Quit' to identify himself, we at Site 18 made our call of KA9WH into King Arthur's Nine Wild Horses.

The call-sign was the only KA9 in existence and it generated a small side story: Call-signs were allocated by the FCC and Stateside ham stations all began with either W or K.

The next letter or number in an American call-sign identified it as located in a particular region in the United States, or else was a military station in a particular country. The second letter, A , was for Japan.

The third part of an overseas military ham call-sign identified the specific area of a country overseas. The number, 9 , was for Hokkaido.

The last two letters usually were the initials of the person who applied for the FCC license. The W H came from the initials of Major William Haines.

(Later when I started a MARS station at Misawa Air Base the FCC gave the 511th station the call-sign of KA8RW.)

That little sidelight about the call-sign lead to the popularity of KA9WH because hams the world over collect and send postcards to each other acknowledging the contact after a communication, and many like to collect rare call-sign cards.

The postcards are called QSL cards, so-named from a 3-letter Q-signal code that has the same meaning to all hams worldwide in all languages. QSL meant 'I communicated with _____ on _____ (and so on).'

The QSL postcards often had cartoons, snapshots and a brief summary about the ham and his radio equipment. Hams would collect them and often tack them on the wall in their ham shack in their attic, cellar, spare room, or garage. The rare QSL cards might include surreptitious ham stations behind the Iron Curtain, or hams at sea, usually radiomen on merchant ships.

(One time I had a CW contact with Captain Kurt Carlson as he was crossing the Pacific. He was the famous captain of the cargo ship Flying Enterprise that broke up in a storm in the Atlantic two years prior. It was a famous sea saga as all the thirty-man crew abandoned ship in the storm and most were rescued. Carlson stayed alone with the ship, resulting in days of worldwide stories and photos before the vessel sank while being towed to England.)

Since collecting QSL cards was part of the hobby of ham radio, and the more rare the better, it follows that a station with K-A-9 would perk up some ears when there were no other K-A-9's.

We were the only KA9 in existence so we were popular with the QSL collectors who called just to ask to please send them a QSL card. So we had some QSL's printed and mailed out a lot.

(One ham in particular stands out. He was in his car using a 10-watt mobile transmitter while parked on top of a mountain in Arizona. His little signal made it all the way to Site 18 because the skip distance was perfect for a short while. 'Skip distance' is the term used to designate signal strength of distant contacts. It comes from radio waves bouncing off the ionosphere and skipping along, bouncing up and down until they peter out.

(When the skip distance was 'right', the signals between two distant locations were loud and clear. They might stay that way for minutes or hours then fade away. Sometimes the skip was perfect every day at the same time for awhile and other times we couldn't catch a good skip for days at a time. A common question among hams was how's the skip today?

(This day the skip was perfect between Site 18 and a mountain in Arizona where a guy sat in his car with his 10-watt mobile rig. He heard me with my 2000 watts and he called me. I called him back and he yelled happily into his microphone, asking would I please please please send him a QSL because no one would ever believe that he had talked from his car radio in Arizona to an Air Force station in Japan. He also said my signal was blowing out his car speakers. Shortly his signal disappeared and I could not hear him. I then looked up his call-sign in the QSL book and sent him a QSL card as proof to his friends).

~~~

Within a few months of operating the MARS station at Site 18 the major rotated home and I transferred to Misawa. Flip and two licensed hams were left, and continued to handle phone patches and radiograms until they rotated home too. Flip left in May of 1954 and the fate of station after that is unknown.

In Misawa, I lived in the transient barracks and saw guys from 18 trickling through on their way home who kept me up-to-date on the MARS station. But I did not hear of any new guys getting licenses. I think that when Flip and the others with licenses rotated home the station went off the air, unless someone from First Radio across the road kept it going.

Or maybe it quietly shut down.

…just as we shut down when the skip distance changed.

~~~~~~

Epilogue

It was fun while it lasted. On a personal note, the six months I was involved with the MARS station at Site 18 changed my remaining time in the Air Force.

Because I now had an FCC ham radio license with the FCC authority to put a MARS station on the air, I was transferred to Misawa to set up a MARS station at 511th Headquarters.

I did that, got a new station on the air (KA8RW), and spent ten months sending and receiving radiograms (mostly relays from Korea) and making phone patches from the 511th station and the well-established Misawa Air Base MARS station.

I didn't have a boss and I lived in a transient barracks. I worked with one technical guy in the 511th who did most of the work to get KA8RW up and running, and a master sergeant at the base station, KA8AB, who had been operating it all by himself.

I made myself scarce and was pretty much on my own with no set schedule. No one knew who I was, or where I was, or where I worked - which was fine by me.

But in reality I spent long and unscheduled hours on the air at the two MARS stations handling traffic and phone patches. It was now a hobby and I enjoyed operating as much as I could. One time I was on the air for twenty-four hours straight.

During that ten month period at Misawa I also played football and baseball for the base teams until I rotated home.

…Not bad duty.

...and just what the hell do you want?

95

Misawa Football

This little tale centers around a football coach.

It does so because it has been said by many that of all sports and more than any other, it is in football that the coach exerts the most influence and makes the most difference.

So here is a story about Captain Julius B. Battista, head coach of the 1953 Misawa Air Base football team at Misawa, Honshu, Northern Japan.

~~~

During the Korean War there was a 12-team Air Force Japan Football League consisting mostly of teams from the Air Force plus a few from the Navy. There were also four non-league teams from the Army. All branches of the service played each other – but most games were between Air Force teams.

The league had two conferences and Misawa won the Northern Conference and Nagoya won the Southern Conference.

The two conference champs then played for bragging rights and the league championship in a game called the Bara Bowl (a word that means 'rose' in Japanese). The game was played on Nagoya's home field and in a tough defensive battle, Nagoya won, 6 to 0.

I was on the Misawa team as an anonymous bench-warmer so my role does not enter the story. This is all about the coach and the team, and I was just more-or-less an active observer.

At the time I was an enlisted man with two stripes and a job as a radio operator. In September I had been transferred to Misawa from Site 18 with orders to set up a MARS Station, the term used for a Military Auxiliary Radio System, also known as ham radio.

Once there I looked up Frank Ciarniello, a friend from Site 18 who transferred to Misawa to play football. Frank had answered the call when Misawa sent word to base organizations, including the remote radar sites on Hokkaido, for football players who could be spared the time off to play for the base team.

Frank jumped at it, knew there was an extra guy for his radar job at Site 18 and was allowed to transfer. I think he also wanted to escape another long, cold, snowy winter in Wakkanai at the top of Hokkaido.

When I saw Frank the season had already started and I had no thought of playing football. But he suggested that I try out for the team since they were short of players at some practices. What he didn't tell me was the need by the team for some new blocking and tackling dummies to beat up on.

I had a flexible schedule since another guy and I were spending our days scrounging for radio equipment for the MARS station. So I tried out for the football team and made it. It was no big deal because I'm sure they gave me a uniform and a big go-get-em-tiger slap on the back to help satisfy the team need for more warm bodies in the full-contact practices.

In my case, and using it as an excuse of course, I was listed as a third-string quarterback, and I spent most of my time at practice as a middle linebacker, an odd position for a quarterback since most quarterbacks played safety on defense in those days. But playing linebacker was more to my liking and limited talent than throwing passes as a quarterback.

My Misawa football career, such as it was, was also influenced in part by the football substitution rules and limitations in effect in the early 1950's.

Those limitations caused players to play both offense and defense, and if a player didn't start he didn't play much or at all during games. The rules also caused juggling by the coaches to get players in and out of games without penalties when a player was injured.

This was before free substitution, and there was not an excess number of players. Many teams might have had more players if they were available but some may have been disallowed since military jobs took precedence.

So, I spent most of my game time on Saturdays way down there at the end of the bench huddled and shivering in my parka with other members of the third string. And spent a lot of time weekdays playing linebacker in practice scrimmages, loving every minute of it. ...That's my story and I'm sticking with it. Cough.

~~~

The brand and caliber of football was plain, nothing fancy. It was better than high school and may have been on a par with second or third tier college ball. Play was spirited, and rough and tough - but clean.

On offense we had only a dozen or so plays using the old T-formation, and a few plays from the new-fangled Split-T.

On defense there were just two formations: the 5-3-2-1 and the 6-2-2-1. It was all very basic in all respects on both sides of the ball. To use a different phrase, it was what it was.

~~~

We had full-contact scrimmages two or three days a week. They lasted a couple of hours at a time and went on week after week. It was physically demanding but I enjoyed banging heads in the all-out wars so for me it was fun. I was a player on the scout team, along for the ride and having a ball.

~~~

Back to the real story of that team: the coach...

Captain Battista, a former line coach at the University of Florida, was of average size, stocky and in his late thirties. He was almost unnoticeable in appearance and his demeanor was one of quiet confidence that easily engendered respect. He had a deep, gravelly voice that could readily be distinguished and recognized during the noise of practice or games, yet he never yelled at players in a screaming way that lesser coaches do.

However, he could get his points across in a manner that convinced players to learn and not repeat mistakes.

When teaching or correcting any player or players he had a sort of impatient growl or a sneer in his voice and a scowl on his face. Quite often his visage was that of a person who had just stepped into something he did not want to step into and now had to scrape that something off his shoes. I'm not sure anyone ever saw him smile, and certainly no one ever heard him laugh.

Believing that repetition was required with this diverse bunch of young football players and wannabees he had two commands he growled over and over, usually spoken in groups of three, as in:

GANG TACKLE!.....GANG TACKLE!.....GANG TACKLE!
and
BLOCK!.....BLOCK!.....BLOCK!

Those commands he repeated constantly, and of course with a snarl or growl. But Captain Battista hardly ever swore. When he did cuss it was just a mild vulgarity, a fact that was a bit surprising given the atmosphere of the few dozen boisterous young guys active on the playing field and in the locker room.

Perhaps more important was Captain Battista's selective use of his favorite and unique words that made everyone snap to a focused alert status with hairs standing on end inside helmets.

When he snarled those unusual words, we cringed.

~~~

Captain Battista was easily the best coach any of us had ever had. To go along with his extensive football knowledge, he had mastered the psychology and art of handling individuals while at the same time building a team from scratch.

Some players he talked to quietly; some he snarled at; some he cajoled; some he was pleasant to; some he picked on over and over; and some he ignored and just let them play. The contrast was interesting to see as he seemed to know which button to push on which player.

Before every game he said the opponent was the best Misawa would face so far. Also before every game he said he knew we could beat them.

The result of his teaching and use of psychology was that he got everyone on same page and to play the best football any had ever played in his life. If a guy had any football ability he found it, got it out of him, expanded it, polished it, and got it out onto the field.

~~~

All the while, of course, the team hated the s.o.b.

He was relentless on physical conditioning, repetitive plays, and contact scrimmages. There often was grumbling in the ranks but everyone went along with it, however reluctantly.   ...It was better than working.

We exercised so much that we were in better condition than anyone we played, and we practiced over and over until everything came naturally and automatically. To reach those points Captain Battista never let up.

Calisthenics were hard and vigorous. To distract us from the drudgery of exercises, he had everyone scream as if in pain as we exercised every day. That made the yelling from the football field during calisthenics sound like dozens of guys being tortured. We weren't, but if anyone was laughing or fooling around then the calisthenics were extended. He also liked to say that if we weren't in pain we were not doing the exercises correctly.

(A couple months after the football season Ciarniello and I played for the Misawa baseball team. During spring training at Nagoya, we caused a lot of turning of heads and quizzical looks as Frank and I yelled and screamed in 'pain' out of football habit during the baseball calisthenics – even though we were in better shape than anyone there.)

One exercise we hated was when he growled 'front' or 'left' or 'right' or 'back' as we were jogging in-place. When 'front' or 'left' or 'right' or 'back' was yelled we had to dive forward or sideways or backward onto the ground without the natural and automatic reaction of using our arms or hands to break our fall.

The worst was 'front' where we had to dive face-first. We did not have face masks on our helmets so the 'front' dive was made worse by the taste of grass and dirt.

Concerning helmets and pads, his rule was that full pads and helmets were to be worn at all times outside the locker room. No one was allowed to take off his helmet in practice or while sitting on the bench during a game. His theory was that constant wearing made the pads and helmets light and unnoticed, therefore no distraction while playing. As usual, he was right.

~~~

The practice scrimmages were wars between the scrubs on the scout team and the starters. Some of us scrubs told the starters that the only reason that Misawa won the conference was because practice against us scrubs was more of a test for the starters than any team they faced. It wasn't true, of course, but the competitive spirit was alive and well between the starters and the rest of us.

~~~

The team consisted mostly of high school players and only a few had any college football experience. Other teams, according to their publicity, had more than we did. We figured that anyone who had played in college was plucked out of line on arrival in Japan and assigned to bases down south. We could not prove that special selection process but the southern teams did have more college players than Misawa did.

~~~

Everyone on the Misawa team was young; except two gray-beards who were all of 24 years old. Our average age was 21, with a few at 19. I don't think there was an officer on the team, and most of us enlisted men had only two stripes. But no one paid attention to the military rank of anyone because football was all that mattered.

On game days we got copies of the game program so we looked up our heights and weights and that of the other team. We wanted to see the intimidation game played by all teams using exaggerated program sizes. For example, I was usually listed an inch taller and ten pounds heavier than I was.

Even with the questionable numbers on game programs, we were still a small team. In the Bara Bowl game we had only one guy listed at over 200 pounds, and just barely at 206, while Nagoya had six guys listed from 205 to 245 pounds.

But if anyone commented about the size difference of teams, Captain Battista would just shrug it off with a so what? He was okay with the discrepancy because his game emphasized speed and conditioning. He would not let team size be a factor in anyone's thinking, saying it was the fight in the dog and not the dog in the fight. Size didn't matter to him and his attitude became the team attitude.

We didn't have the biggest team in any of the games but we did have a bunch of young jocks who liked to play football with some talent and a whole lot of spirit. We also had a secret weapon in Captain Battista.

~~~

Misawa's best player was Roy Hina, an all-star tackle. Roy was listed at 5'11' and 182 pounds, which I think was stretching it a bit, especially because he played both offensive and defensive tackle.

He was very fast and very good, and he had to be very fast and very good with his relatively small size because of the position he played. As 'small' as he was, Roy played opposite the biggest guys on the other teams and did so very successfully. Beside his all-star talent he was probably the nicest guy on the team.

Injuries were a fact of life in football, and it didn't help that we did not have face masks. In the early 1950's face masks were just starting to be used and most of us had not used them back home.

We did not have face masks at Misawa but some other teams did, so the wearing of a face mask was a conversation topic among the players. In general the consensus was that most preferred to play without them, and all were extra careful when playing against teams that had them.

There was fear that a face mask could be grabbed inadvertently and twisted in the speed of the action, and could result in a broken neck. If given the choice, most would have chosen to play without face masks, preferring bruises and maybe a broken nose or broken tooth to a broken neck.

~~~

Captain Battista's attitude toward injuries was unique in that he appeared not to care if someone got hurt, as often someone did in the full speed scrimmages.

A couple of times when an injured player got hurt in practice and could not get himself up off the ground and off to the side to recover or for treatment, the captain said, "Ok, move the ball over; we'll play over here." Sympathy wasn't part of his scene.

One halfback had a hairline fracture in his foot near the end of the season, didn't know it, and continued to play in pain. He filled up on A.P.C.'s, the famous All Purpose Cure that was only aspirin, and forced himself to limp as little as possible. He did not know that he had a hairline fracture; he just knew his foot hurt badly.

He said that he sure as hell was not going to say anything to the captain in fear of being called a weakling or worse for not playing in pain. And he said that he knew if he went to the hospital and they found something serious they would not let him play. So he skipped practices, saying he had to work, concealed his limp as much as he could and played in the last couple of games.

After the bowl game his foot was x-rayed, the hairline fracture found, a cast put on and he was given crutches. When he showed up on crutches at the break-up banquet at the end of the season Captain Battista was amazed, as were many on the team. Few knew that he had played the last two games with more than just a sore foot.

The captain said he hadn't known, felt very badly and told him how he admired the guy for playing hurt. At that the half-back was satisfied that finally he had the captain's respect.

~~~

As noted earlier, Captain Battista did not really swear or cuss although he did use mild vulgarities now and then. But he did have two sets of unusual words that he used as emphasis and to get our attention. One had two words and the other four words.

If we heard either we really hoped it was directed at someone else as we tried to shrink inside our helmets and uniforms or wish ourselves invisible. The first set of words that made our hair stand on end were

snail shit.

That indicated that Captain Battista was unhappy and he was about to make a player very unhappy by getting into his face to discuss the error of his ways.

After the growled lesson that indicated and corrected a

mistake it was often requested by the snarling Captain Battista that the errant player run a 200-plus-yard lap around the goalposts or to drop down and do at least ten push-ups in football uniform.

The other set of words used by our non-swearing coach was

hog's ass and garlic.

That was classic. We never could figure out its meaning or derivative but it always created a bunch of sighs and murmurs from players. And those murmurs from the players were not 'aw shucks' or 'jiminy cricket'.

Hog's ass and garlic was used more often in a team sense in that it usually indicated that a whole bunch of players just didn't get it.

...It is entirely possible to picture Captain Battista restlessly on the sideline during a game or standing near the action in a practice and muttering to himself just how did anyone expect him to get results from this bunch of misfits. Snail shit.

The epithets were funny in their stand-alone way, but when Captain Battista growled either the individual or team reaction was ...oh-oh, now what? who screwed up? hope it wasn't me...

'Snail shit' or 'hog's ass and garlic' could be heard through the noise and din of practice or a game, no one dared smile unless it was out of the captain's vision; and no one dared make fun of it in case the captain noticed and suggested a bunch of push-ups or goalpost laps.

~~~

During the season, and especially when it looked like Misawa had a shot at the championship, the base newspaper published articles that helped to generate football interest throughout the sprawling air base. The winning season and championship race was good for morale.

After the Bara Bowl the big brass of Misawa Air Base gave a banquet honoring the team. It was a pretty big deal and on the program were listed names and ranks of 42 honored guests and details about 41 team members, with the following summary

42 Honored Guests:

1 general, 9 bird colonels, 10 light colonels,
4 majors, 2 captains, 3 lieutenants,
1 warrant officer, 10 sergeants, 2 civilians.

~~~

41 Team Members:

1 coach, 2 assistant coaches, 1 doctor,
2 managers, 35 players.

It was not clear to the team what the honored guests had to do with the football team or what they were being honored for.

Aside from the extensive listing of names on the program at the banquet there were dozens of attendees and fans. There also were speeches honoring the team, acknowledging morale boost and interest on the big air base by the team's success.

General Grant lead the banquet followed by Colonel Pardy and Colonel Sherwood. Each team member got a personalized program with his name on it at his assigned seat, and after the meal and speeches, each team member was introduced individually and given an engraved statuette of a football player about to throw a pass. The engraving on the statuette is

Northern Conference Champions

1953 Bara Bowl Runnerup

~~~

Later, the team had its own private break-up meeting and each member of the team received separate Letters of Appreciation from Colonel Pardy and Colonel Sherwood. Everyone was also given a sports jacket embroidered

Northern Conference Champions
Misawa Air Base Football
1953

Then everyone crammed into, or tried to cram into, the office used by Captain Battista. It was a small classroom with a dozen chairs and a large blackboard.

The players sprawled in the chairs or stood around the room and spilled out the door while Captain Battista sat at his desk.

A couple of guys made humorous thank you speeches as the team laughed and clapped.

The noisy scene was climaxed by a gift of an engraved writing pen desk-set presented to Captain Battista by the team captain, Roy Hina, who read aloud the engraving:

to
Captain Julius B. Battista

from
Misawa Air Base Thunderjets

Northern Conference Football Champions
Japan,   1953

~~~
S.S.,   H.A. and G.

</div>

Captain Battista smiled and stood up at his desk. If the players didn't know better some might have thought his eyes welled up a skoshe...naw, he's not sentimental. Not him.

But he was surprised and he was at a loss for words.

He stammered something not heard by all as he stood there looking down at the engraving on the desk-set while the whole team roared and clapped.

Voices of team members around the room were heard to mutter or yell out comments that included the famous words hog's ass and garlic, plus, of course, snail shit.

Then more raucous laughter.

Captain Battista had built a football team from scratch, the team had a good season, and now it was over.

...Snail shit.

<div align="center">

~~~~~~

109

Misawa Football Team – 1953

Head Coach	J. Battista	Gainesville, FL
Asst. Coach	Bill Edwards	Dallas, TX
Asst. Coach	Warren Kilway	Akron, OH
Team Doctor	Bill Dowling	San Francisco, CA
Manager	Joe DePaul	Conshohoken, PA
Manager	Henry Bowling	Nashville, TN

no.	pos.	ht.	wt.	age	name	hometown
20	QB	5'8	158	22	Frank Ciarniello	Youngstown, OH
22	E	5'11	168	19	Jackie Hudson	Chicago, IL
24	HB	5'9	157	21	Larry Turner	Lake View, IA
25	HB	5'10	177	23	Walt Ackerman	Burlingame, CA
30	HB	6'1	177	21	Wilbur Pack	Pauls Valley, OK
31	FB	5'8	173	22	Jack Coates	Osona, TX
32	HB	5'8	153	21	Gene Fritz	Knoxville, TN
33	FB	5'10	177	20	Art Collier	Brookfield, MO
34	G	5'10	161	22	Dick Wood	Allentown, PA
36	E	5'10	189	23	Fred Horton	East Orange, NJ
37	HB	5'10	167	21	Harold Schlagel	Garfield, OH
38	E	6'2	193	22	Cal Leonard	Spartanburg, SC
39	E	6'1	178	23	Bill Taylor	Pensacola, FL
41	E	5'11	180	22	Len Vannucci	Pittsburg, PA
42	QB	6'0	172	21	Dick Waldron	Roslindale, MA
43	T	5'11	182	24	Roy Hina	Sturgis, KY
44	FB	5'11	173	22	Don Shetter	Atlanta, GA
45	QB	6'1	180	19	John Stuart	Greensboro, NC
46	G	5'10	187	21	Ron Bestow	Mattson, IL
47	G	6'0	195	22	Robin Howell	Oak Harbor, WA
48	T	6'1	196	23	Jimmy Ryan	Buffalo, NY
49	T	6'1	198	20	Sam Coen	Altoona, PA
50	G	6'1	188	20	Jack Atwood	Burbank, CA
51	T	6'1	190	20	Carl Baker	Aurora, IL
52	E	6'1	190	22	George Vest	Columbus, OH
55	G	5'11	193	19	Bob Heard	Miami, FL
56	T	6'0	198	24	Art Escude	Columbus, OH
58	C	5'10	206	21	Dale Nelson	Rock Island, IL
59	G	5'10	188	22	Tom Dragna	Burbank, CA

The detailed list on the previous page is from the game program at the:

Bara Bowl

AF Japan Championship Game

Misawa A.B. vs. Nagoya A.B.

5 DEC 53   1330 Hours

Mizuho Stadium, Nagoya, Japan

~~~~~~

Additional players listed (no details) on the banquet program:

Misawa Air Force Base Football Banquet

Honoring

**The Air Force Japan Northern Conference
Champions**

1953

Jack Beaudry
Bruce Brown
Bob Coblentz
Joe Marshall
Ralph Medeffesser

~~~~~~

1953 Misawa AB Conference Champions

1953 Misawa AB Football Team - Northern Conference Champions

------

top row: Robin Howell, Bill Taylor, Carl Baker, Dale Nelson

4th row: Dick Wood, Don Shetter, John Stuart, Jackie Hudson,
Art Collier, Gene Fritz, Walt Ackerman

3rd row: Cal Leonard, Ben Lawrence, Larry Turner, Fred Horton,
Jimmie Ryan, Jack Coates, George Clay

2nd row: Dick Waldron, Frank Ciarniello, Dom Dicenzeo,
Wilbur Pack, Harold Schlegel, Ron Bestow, George Vest

1st row: Bob Heard, Tom Dragna, Jack Atwood, Len Vannucci,
Sam Coen, Art Escude, Roy Hina (team captain)

players not in photo: Jack Beaudry, Bruce Brown, Bob Coblentz,
Joe Marshall, Ralph Medeffessor

others: J. Battista (Head Coach);
Bill Edwards and Warren Kilway (Assistant Coaches);
Bill Dowling (Team Doctor);
Joe DePaul and Henry Bowling (Team Managers)

113

Descriptions

DF / The Lodge / Nob Hill

DF was the abbreviation for direction finding equipment used for navigation information with aircraft. At Site 18, DF contact was infrequent but there were F-86 fighters patrolling Hokkaido, L-20 courier planes visiting sites, and RB-29 spy planes that, according to published newspaper stories, flew over the Russia mainland and the island, Sakhalin, north of Hokkaido.

(Sakhalin was a Japanese island occupied by the Russia at the end of WWII. Russia changed the big island's name to Sakhalin from Karafuto, the Japanese name. Newspaper reports used both names in articles about American RB-29's attacked by Russian MIGs and Russian aircraft attacked by American F-86's.)

There were Russian air bases on Sakhalin and occasionally MIGs flew over Site 18 just to buzz the site and then go home. One time we heard a Russian pilot swear at us in English on the monitored voice frequency, then heard him laugh before roaring very low over the site and heading back north to his base as we shook our fists and swore at him in response.

DF equipment was small and required little space. The first DF shack at Site 18 was less than ten feet long and maybe five feet wide. The shack was tiny, and beside DF equipment, it just had room for an electric space heater, a hot plate, and a chair.

That shack, on the edge of the cliff behind the site, was reached by climbing slowly up a very steep path, which was slippery in bad weather. We had to haul ourselves up the cliff by pulling on a rope hand over hand, with sandwiches, C-rations and reading material in a bag over one shoulder - not an easy feat in winter with snow.

At the DF shack there was just one radio operator and a shift was twelve hours, either all day or all night. Both shifts dragged. Thankfully that DF location did not last long, and in 1952 a new shack was built two miles away.

The new DF location was reached by tracked vehicles over a winding dirt road worn into existence by vehicles bringing equipment to create the site. A bulldozer was used to help carve a road out of the bare hills and flatten a hilltop. The dirt road always was either muddy or snow-covered, and getting there and back was an adventure with the pot holes and bumps. Sometimes the driver of the weasel skipped the road and used the fields to get there.

The new building was a Quonset hut big enough for a bunk on each side, a table in the middle, a pot-bellied oil stove, and the DF equipment. At least it had a little elbow room. There was also a 10'x10' utility shed for the diesel power unit. After the cramped conditions on the edge of the cliff, this was luxurious. It was therefore named The Lodge.

With living conditions improved and travel time increased to a half hour or more, the shifts at The Lodge were expanded to two radio operators in shifts of 24-on and 24-off, and instead of scaling a cliff to DF a ride to The Lodge was given by tracked weasel.

A few months later, when the novelty wore off but the austere living conditions remained, The Lodge was renamed. With tongue-in-cheek it became Nob Hill, the wealthy enclave in San Francisco.

And so Nob Hill, the name given in irony to a small, isolated DF Quonset hut on top of a hill two miles from anywhere, would be on the air and called Nob Hill by the troops for years to come.

Weather Reports

Weather reports were required to be sent every three hours from Site 18 to Misawa Air Base, and most likely from other sites as well.

At 18, the reports were handled by the radio operators who filled out the preprinted form in the special five-number code and sequence required, and sent the messages via Morse Code.

These reports were used in planning spy flights over Russian territory by RB-29's, the spy planes used by the U.S. before the U-2. The reports were also used by F-86 patrol flights around Hokkaido as well as the occasional L-20 courier planes.

So far, so good. However, the only weather instrument available was a thermometer attached outside the window. Beside the temperature the report called for the barometric pressure, precipitation (snow or rain, heavy or light,), wind (direction and velocity), cloud cover (clear or percentage), and visibility (miles).

That's asking a lot from a plain old window thermometer. So some ingenuity and imagination was needed.   ...Call it guessing.

Outside the one radio room window were sand bags piled high on top of sand filled barrels a few feet away from the building. At one end where the wall of barrels and sand bags ended a limited view of the outside world could be seen.

This truncated view included a few hundred square feet of open space outside the motor pool, a small patch of grass not destroyed by vehicles, and a slice of the sky.

Looking out that window was the procedure for making out the important weather reports. And this made radiomen uneasy knowing that their guesswork could affect flight plans and pilot and crew safety.

The radio operator looked out the window, saw which way the wind was blowing by the direction the snow was moving or the grass was bending, guessed the wind speed, saw if it was snowing or raining, determined if light or heavy precipitation, looked up at the slice of sky to estimate cloud cover (tricky at night but guessed by the sight of stars or not) and read the one weather instrument, the outside thermometer. At night these guesswork reports were usually skipped as impossible.

From those bits of observation (cough), the radioman made out the weather report and sent it by Morse Code to Misawa.

That sequence every three hours when possible meant that the only time a weather report was accurate was when visibility was zero due to howling and swirling winds with blowing snow. That combination produced blanks in the weather report except for temperature, snow and zero visibility.

Later the reports were handled by the radar folks a mile away on Hilltop who, it was hoped, had more equipment to work with.

But before radar personnel took over, radio operators were the weathermen without instruments who produced detailed weather reports every three hours by looking out the window.

The reports had to be used by pilots and flight planners, and radio operators were uneasy knowing that others relied on such detailed information known to be a W.A.G. - wild ass guess.

RB-29 photo recon spy plane circling Site 18.

21-Gun Salute

The photograph says it all.

It is a picture of enlisted men mostly in fatigues and a mixed assortment of informal clothing lined up opposite each other on a dirt road and each, except one, carrying a carbine.

Some are lined up shooting the carbines in unison into the air, some are in process of lining up their carbines to shoot into the air, some have already shot their carbines into the air, and some are a few beats behind the others.

There are about ten men on one side of the road and about eight men on the other. The photograph is unclear because some are slightly behind others. A couple of men in khakis without weapons are shown with their backs to the camera and one was probably giving the orders to ready, aim, fire.

There is at least one guy on the near right who is fiddling with a handgun, which may be a .45, but later word went around that it might have been something else. At the time I wrote a letter home calling the brief minutes a 21 ½ gun salute, with the ½ gun a small Japanese pistol.

At the far end and in the center of the picture is a parked jeep at an angle showing Major Haines looking out at the goings-on. He and some others are wearing their cowboy hats from the recent horseback inspection.

The occasion was the day that Major Haines rotated home after serving about six months as commanding officer of Site 18.

The guys thought it would be nice to show their appreciation for his attitude and approach by giving him a 21-gun salute. No particular reason: everyone just liked the guy.

Over a third of the 60 personnel on the site at the time were on duty and the number for the salute did not quite get to 21.But the intent remained, and it was spontaneous. A sudden idea was met with an enthusiastic response of ...hey, let's do it!

The picture also illustrates the informal atmosphere yet the togetherness that existed among the men. The idea on the site was to get the job done but don't sweat the military stuff.

The day Major Haines went home was a day to remember with a smile because of the '21-gun salute.' No one knew the rules but it didn't matter. Nor did it matter that there were not 21 guns or that everyone was dressed informally.

As Shakespeare or somebody said, the king was dead, long live the king. The major's short time at the site had ended; the informal life on the site continued.

But life as we knew it couldn't last as the size and numbers of personnel grew in the coming months from sixty young men to hundreds, which changed everything.

What did not change were the memories.

Like the time the major went home and we gave him a 21-gun salute. Or close to it.

Proof is in the unofficial Air Force photograph.

21 Gun Salute

First Radio Security Service &
the University of Massachusetts

... A little side story: After I was discharged from the Air Force I went to the University of Massachusetts at Amherst.

In my senior year, 1959, I got kicked out of a dormitory and off campus for cooking with a hot plate in my dorm room.

So I moved into a rooming house downtown where there were a half dozen other ex-GI's who had trouble with dorm rules.

At the rooming house the following conversation took place. It was between my new roommate and me:

me: " ... so you were in the Air Force, huh?"
him: " Yeah."
me: " What was your job?"
him: " I was a radio operator."
me: " Really! So was I. Where were you stationed?"
him: " In Japan."
me: " Yeah, when?"
him: " 52 to 54."
me: " That was the same time I was over there. Whereabouts?"
him: " Up north."
me: " So was I; where up north?"
him: " On Hokkaido, at Wakkanai."
me: " So was I !! But I don't remember you. We must have been there at different times. Were you at the radar site?"
him: " Nope. I was in First Radio across the road."
me: " Well, how about that. Here it is, five years later, and we meet in a rooming house at UMass and find out we were stationed practically at the same place in Japan at the same time but never met."

126

him: " Ya, how about that."

me: " I dunno why but we never mixed with you guys. You did your thing and we did ours."

him: " Right."

me: " I know I never crossed the road onto the First Radio site and I don't think I ever saw any of you guys on our site."

him: " Uh-huh."

me: " All we knew was that you listened to a lot of Morse Code coming from Russia or Karafuto while we watched things on radar. By the way, what were you guys monitoring?"

him: " Can't tell you."

me: " Huh? Why not? "

him: " Can't tell you."

me: " That's ridiculous. The Korean War is over and done with. It's been five years. It's history. And you can't say what you were doing in Japan five years ago? What's that all about? Why the big secret five years later?"

him: " Can't tell you."

And he walked away.

…So much for 'war stories' and one college roommate. The arms-length relationship between First Radio and Site 18 would go on for years after the two small, unrelated Air Force outfits were neighbors separated by a dirt road. There was very little contact or socializing between the two outfits. They were all radio, we were radio and radar. And rarely did one speak to the other, and fewer still crossed the road in either direction. I heard we swapped movies occasionally but I never knew anyone to actually visit either side.

Five years later two of us were roommates, one from Site 18 and the other from First Radio Security Service across the road, but I don't think we ever had a second conversation. Each of us apparently chose to study and drink beer at different places.

Photographs

Site 18 from a very high radio antenna pole.

How cold was it? Well, cold enough to affect the anatomy of a brass monkey, and to crack plastic windows on a weasel.

Mess hall ladies: Hedy, Aiko, Peggy.

Tourists checking out Honeybucket Sam's rig and ladle. (Dick Waldron, Al Setting, Grover Ashcraft, Bob Gray)

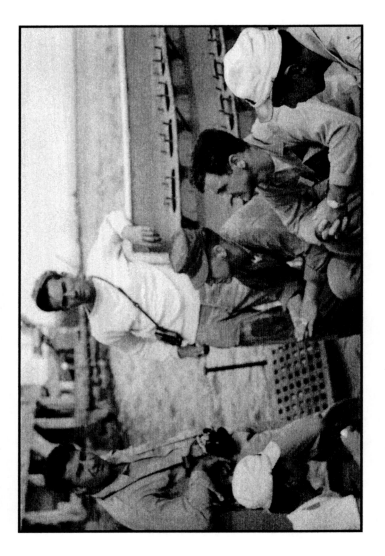

Visitors on a Japanese patrol boat that intercepted and
had a shootout with some Russian smugglers or spies.
(Al Setting, Paul Sheehan, Joe Hennessey, Reno Giuntoli)

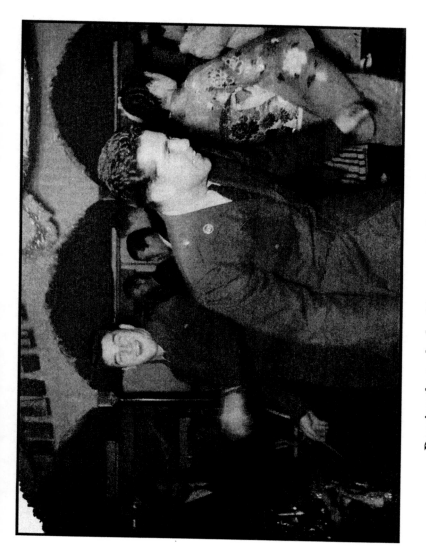

Dancing the tonka-bushi - guess who is out of step.

135

Step right up, guess your mileage, win a trip home.

The Golden Gate Bridge

137

Site 18 Alumni at the Nashville reunion in 1998.

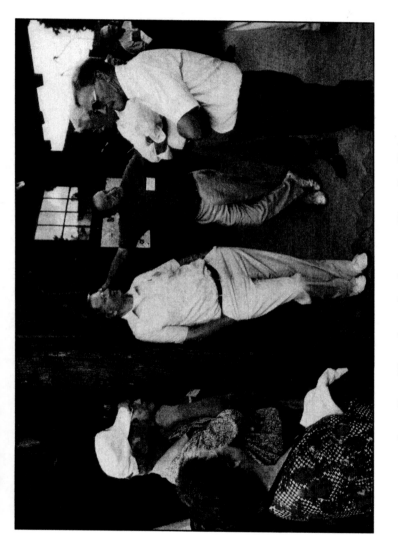

So, tell us, Tim, then what happened?   ...Really?

139

Newspaper Articles

****

Newspaper Article #1:

The New York Times
March 1, 1951

KURILE ISSUE IN DOUBT

... Mr. Dulles also hinted that the Soviet Union's occupation of South Sakhalin and the Kurile Islands, authorized by the Yalta agreement, probably would not be recognized if Moscow snubbed the treaty settlement.

A situation described as an aggravation already has arisen, Mr. Dulles said, with respect to the Russian occupation of the tiny Habomai group of islands just off the northern coast of Hokkaido, the northern island of Japan.

The two largest units of the Habomai group are only a few acres in size, and rise to about thirty feet above sea level. The Soviet Union occupied them at the end of the last war, on the understanding, apparently, that they were part of the Kuriles. This understanding, according to Mr. Dulles, is disputed by the United States which contends that the Habomai Islands never have been historically treated as part of the Kuriles.

The National Geographic Society noted in a statement tonight that "it takes a considerable stretch of the imagination to construe them as belonging to the Kurile Islands chain.

Mr. Dulles cited a letter he had received from General Mac-Arthur – a letter Mr. Dulles said he thought paid "a very precious tribute to the effort we were making in Japan."

General MacArthur wrote:

"I'm confident that the influence of the peace formula we seek for Japan will extend far beyond the immediate problem it seeks to solve. For a peace based upon such high concepts of justice and right designed to erase the scars of war and restore the vanquished to a position of dignity and equality among nations presents a new spiritual idea to mankind and evokes new standards of morality in international relations."

142

Newspaper Article # 2:

The New York Times
December 5, 1951

U.S. UNIT ON HOKKAIDO CLOSE TO SOVIET SOIL

SOMEWHERE ON HOKKAIDO, Japan,
Wednesday, December 5, 1951

Several hundred Americans are staring down the throats of the Russians on this mountainous, snow-covered island.

They are Air Force personnel who operate the radar network spread across this closest point to Russia proper. They are part of the island defense the United States is pledged to maintain.

Hokkaido's 34,267 square miles lies in the most critical area of possible Communist attack in event of a third world war.

Its southeastern tip is only three miles from the nearest island in the Soviet-dominated Kuriles chain.

The northernmost coastline is twenty-two miles at points from Russia's Sakhalin Island, which extends like a wrench toward a nut Russia may try to turn.

The Russians are so close the land they dominate can be seen clearly on a fair day.

Their ships pass through the narrow straits between Sakhalin and Hokkaido. Soviet planes are picked up on radar screens and sometimes can be sighted visibly. Soviet searchlights play across the skies at night.

~~~~~~

Newspaper Article # 3:

The New York Times
Thursday, October 9, 1952

B-29 Lost Off Soviet Kuriles;

Radar Traces Unidentified Machine
Heading East Into Superfort's Path

Tokyo, Thursday, October 9 - A B-29 Superfort, carrying a
crew of eight, disappeared Tuesday shortly after radar equipment had picked up an unidentified plane approaching it from
the direction of the Kurile Islands, the Far East Air Forces said
today.

The Air Force said the radar tracks of the two planes merged.
It did not say the unidentified plane was Russian or that the
Superfort was attacked. A spokesman said there were no other
United States planes in the area at the time.

With armed Thunderjets flying cover, search planes zig-
zagged over the sea off northern Japan today in a continuing
search for the Superfort. The planes sighted only an oil slick
yesterday. Foul weather hampered the search.

A Far East spokesman said the search would not extend
beyond Japanese territorial waters.

Call in English Heard

The spokesman said a voice distress call in English, presumably
from the bomber, had been heard Tuesday and then a crew
member had shouted: "Let's get the hell out of here!"

The newspaper Asahi said the Japanese police reported that a plane, issuing black smoke, had crashed into the sea near Nemuro, northeast Hokkaido, at about 2:20 P.M. They said the plane fell apparently in a Soviet-controlled area.

The Air Force spokesman refused comment on that report. The Air Force said the Japan-based Superfort was on a routine flight at 15,000 feet and "was under the customary United States radar observation." The radar plot showed it was heading east. The Air force added: "A second but unidentified plane was sighted at about 2:15 P.M. heading westerly about seven miles inside Japanese Territory.

"The tracks of the unidentified aircraft and the B-29 were followed until they merged on the radarscope about eight miles northwest of Nemuro, which point is in Japanese territory about fifteen miles from the international border.

"The merged radar tracks, still over Japanese territory, continued southeast for a few moments and then disappeared from the radar scope. Shortly thereafter, a single unidentified 'May Day' call (voice SOS) was heard, presumably from the Superfort. Then there was silence."

The spokesman said it was possible for two planes in the same general area to merge on a radar scope if they were close together. He said it was possible for a plane to go below the range of the radar line of sight. This could account for the disappearance of the unidentified plane.

Newspaper Article # 4:

(three articles, same edition)

The New York Times
January 22, 1953

HOKKAIDO IS CALM
UNDER SOVIET PROD

U.S. General Reassures People
of Northern Japanese Island
His Forces Will Stay

Sapporo, Hokkaido, Japan, Jan. 21 -- The people of Hokkaido
are not afraid of the Russians, a half-dozen miles across the sea,
as long as American armed forces remain on this northernmost
island of Japan.

Russian flights over Japanese territory and resultant Japanese
and American warnings that such aerial trespassers might be shot
down have not heightened Hokkaido's apprehension over its
Soviet neighbors. The stock comment is, "When you live at the
foot of a volcano you don't worry about lava."

By frequent trips around the islands, some courtesy calls on
mayors and by public statements, the American commander
here, Maj. Gen. Arthur G. Trudeau, has quieted rumors that the
United States forces were pulling out.

The people reason they are safe as long as there is no general
war for, they argue, an attack on Hokkaido is an attack on Japan
and an attack on America, which would bring on World War III.

146

Many Causes For Worry

Yet there are some reasons for the people to be jittery. Not only have Russian planes violated Japanese territory, but Soviet searchlights from land bases and from small cutters are played on Wakkanai and Nemuro.

Japanese authorities believe the Russian actions are the result of tight Soviet security measures around the Kurile Islands.

There are reports of new radar installations on Yuri Island in the Habomai group nearest Japan.

In 1952 the Russians seized thirty-six Japanese fishing boats with 270 fishermen, in the Nemuro area. Of these, twenty-six ships and 203 men have been released. In the Wakkanai area, at the northern tip of the island, ten ships with 114 men were captured and eight ships with 81 men returned.

The fishermen allegedly, and perhaps in reality, violated Russian waters. Sometimes the engines of boats stop and they drift across the line. Sometimes they "lose their way." Sometimes the Japanese have knowingly sailed into Soviet waters, where they believe the catch is richer.

Captives Are Blindfolded

The captured Japanese are blindfolded to prevent observation of Soviet activities once they are ashore in Soviet territory. Jailed and tried, they usually are released unless they are suspected of espionage.

Hokkaido, once a stronghold of Communist agitation, has no Red internal sores now. In the October general elections, the Communists polled only 42,000 votes or one-tenth of 1 per cent of votes in the rest of the country.

147

Japanese Saw B-29 Shot Down

Tokyo, Jan. 21 (AP) -- Japanese fishermen just released from Soviet captivity said today they saw Russian fighter planes and ground guns shoot down a United States B-29 last Oct. 7 off Hokkaido. One fisherman said he saw two Russian fighter planes chase the B-29, heard gunfire and then: "Black smoke started to stream from the American plane and it crashed into the sea at a tremendous speed.

U.S. Jets Chase Strange Lights

United States Air Base, Northern Japan,
Thursday, Jan. 22 (AP)

Strange clusters of red, white and green lights flying at blinding speed have been chased twice by United states jet pilots over northern Japan, the Air Force said Wednesday.

The hurtling, rotating clusters were seen the nights of Dec. 29 and Jan. 9 over northern Honshu, the main island of Japan.

"Frequency of related sightings attest to some unconventional flying object active in this general area." said an Air Force intelligence report on the Dec. 29 spotting, indication the mysterious lights had been seen many times before.

"There are too many indications of the presence of something for the source's remarks to be considered an observation of nothing," it added.

148

Newspaper Article # 5:
(two articles in same edition)

The New York Times
January 23, 1953

SEA AND AIR POWER
HELD HOKKAIDO KEY

General Trudeau Says He Could
Hold Japanese Island With
First Cavalry Division

Sapporo, Hokkaido, Japan, Jan. 22 –

Japan's northernmost island of Hokkaido, facing Soviet
territory on three sides, is being bolstered with additional
Japanese and American military strength.

An attack on Hokkaido would serve a double purpose.
It would trap a substantial segment of the Japanese defense
force and the American Army strength assigned to Japan,
and it would acquire airfields from which fighter planes
could fly against Honshu, Japan's major island.

Military men here agree that in case of an attack the
bulk of any enemy force should be defeated at sea or in
the air before it had a chance to wade ashore or parachute
to land.

Maj. Gen. Arthur G. Trudeau, with the better part of
his First Cavalry Division on the island, likes to compare
Hokkaido with the Island of Luzon in the Philippines. He

has a map of Luzon by his desk at his headquarters four miles outside Sapporo.

Air and Sea Power Seen Key

"Luzon was easier to defend than Hokkaido would be," he said. "The Ishikari Plain is the heart of Hokkaido. It holds the seat of prefectural government, Sapporo, and has all communications. From the Sea of Japan to the Pacific, the Plain is less than fifty miles across.

"Now MacArthur lost his airpower in the first days of the war. Here we have substantial air and naval power. Whether they would be available at the needed time is another question because of the Korean situation. If I could count on full air and naval power I would have few qualms about defending Hokkaido with the few ground forces here."

One potential factor in Hokkaido's defense is the Japanese National Safety Corps – the new national militia. Though General Trudeau said he was impressed by the caliber of the officers and the men he added it would be "impossible to predict what the situation would be regarding the effectiveness or even the availability of the corps" because of the Japanese Constitution outlawing war as an instrument of policy.

There is no unified command on Hokkaido and no exchange of liaison officers.

Japanese Only Lightly Armed

The Japanese force was activated last Oct. 15 and by March will have 30,000 men distributed in several camps. The force is equipped with rifles, mortars and bazookas. It has 155-mm guns and some tanks, but only for training purposes.

The United States Air Force is stationed at Chitosi airfield, a forty-five-minute jeep ride from Sapporo. It keeps a few jets there, but the bulk of the air striking force is on Honshu. It recently acquired some small airfield on Hokkaido, apparently for emergency use.

Maintaining the fighting ability and morale of the First Cavalry has been a major task for General Trudeau. The division had a 100 per cent turnover in one year. Some men served with the division only five months.

The general put the men through a heavy winter training program of snowshoeing, skiing and five-day marches and bivouacs. The accent has been on small unit training.

"The relationship between the troops and the civilian population is the best I have seen in twenty-nine years of service, and that includes the United States," he said. There were less than five Japanese complaints a month against soldiers, he said.

~~~~~~~~~~~~~~~~~~~~~~~~~~~~~~~~

Peiping Hits at Hokkaido Bases

Tokyo, Friday, Jan 23 –

The Peiping radio charged today that Japan had fanned war fever under orders from the United States. The Chinese Communist radio struck back at Japan's recent warning to the Soviet Union against violations of Japanese air by Soviet planes.

A Chinese Red broadcast, heard in Tokyo, said "the American aggressors have turned Hokkaido, which is near Soviet territory, into one of their major military bases in Japan."

Peiping said United States occupation troops had twenty-two military bases in Hokkaido. It said a picked division of Japanese security forces, equipped with heavy arms, was garrisoning the island under United States direction.

"The United States aggressors have always attached importance to Hokkaido in their plans for converting Japan into a springboard of aggression in the Far East." Peiping said.

"United States Occupation troops built military bases in Hokkaido with Sapporo and Chitose as the centers. In Sapporo and Chitose the United States troops have used $30,000,000 for large-scale military construction."

~~~~~~

Newspaper Article Number 6:

(This comes from a two-page pictorial article with fourteen
pictures from various sites and a few sentences of captions
per picture. The article was in *The Wingspread*, the base
newspaper. Below is the column that introduced it.)

~~~

The Wingspread
Misawa Air Base

February 13, 1953

SEEING THE SITES

Just a few hours ride by ferry from here lies the northernmost
island of Japan, Hokkaido - the island that is within seeing
distance of Russian territory, the island where the most strategic
part of the air defense is located: the radar sites.

All these sites, commanded by Colonel George H. Sutherlin,
commanding officer of the 511th AC&W Group, are constantly
on the lookout for hostile aircraft and are charged with the
responsibility of alerting the members of the Northern Defense
Area if ever there is cause to do so.

These sites, located in isolated positions of the icy, bitter
island of Hokkaido are not like our bases here, or down south.

They do not have the movies, the clubs, or the recreational
and athletic facilities that we have. They have nothing but an

isolated area and they are charged with the most important operations of our air defense: radar.

They serve the same tour of duty that the men of the southern bases do but without the extra time off because theirs is a job where all men have to be on the alert at all times, always ready to spread the alarm in case of need.

Tons and tons of snow entrench them in their little locations, and some even have to melt snow to shave.

They have to wait until the first of each month before they can buy any P.X. supplies shipped to them and sold around the pay table.

Their mail comes not daily as at the southern bases, but once a week.

Each unit has but one or perhaps two medics to help in case of need. Often a Japanese doctor is called in case of emergency and this policy is reversed at times. On one of the sites it is known that one of the medics is responsible for the successful delivery of eight Japanese babies when the Japanese doctor could not be reached.

Wherever we are in Japan and whenever we think of the possibilities of attack, we can rest assured that these untiring, patriotic and enduring airmen are aware of our feelings and we will always know when danger threatens our bases.

If it ever should, we can thank them in our hearts for looking out for us with their constant vigil, and the realization of the important job that they do so well.

Newspaper Article # 7:

The New York Times
February 16, 1953

U.S. Jets Gun Soviet-Type Planes Over North Japan; Damaging One

Tokyo, Monday, Feb 16 (AP) –

Two United States jet interceptors fired on two Russian-type fighter planes over Northern Japan today and damaged one in a chase back toward the Kurile Islands, the Far East Air Forces said.

The American planes broke off the chase to "avoid violation of Russian-held territory," F.E.A.F. added. It identified the planes as LA-11's, new Russian 400-mile-an-hour "prop" fighters.

This was the first incident reported since Japan warned recently that she was asking the United States Air Force to prevent unauthorized flights over Japanese territory.

The Air Force said the United States jets were on routine patrol over Hokkaido, northernmost island of Japan, at 11:15 A.M. when ground radar directed them to two "unidentified aircraft flying over Hokkaido and violating Japanese territory.

The F.E.A.F. gave this version of the incident:

"Pursuant to standing instructions, our interceptor pilots signaled the intruders to land.

"The landing signal was ignored by the LA-11 pilots.

"Our leader then opened fire, scoring hits on the fuselage and wings of one of the intruders.

"The intruder aircraft then proceeded toward the Russian-held Kurile Islands. Our pilots broke off the engagement to avoid violation of Russian territory."

The announcement said the United Stated radar operators first spotted the intruding aircraft.

The incident took place near Nemuro, on the eastern tip of Hokkaido and within sight of the Kuriles.

The brief announcement by Gen. O.P. Weyland, Far East Air Forces commander, did not identify the type of United States jet. Previously F.E.A.F. had said that F-86 Sabres, the scourge of the Communist MIG's in Korea, were patrolling Northern Japan.

It was in the same area that a United States B-29 Superfort was shot down Oct. 7. The Soviet Union protested that the B-29 had violated Russian territory and fired first on Soviet planes.

The Air Force said the B-29 "carried no guns and no gunners." The State Department later informed Moscow that the B-29 was not over Soviet territory, charged the Soviet Union with wanton destruction of the plane and warned of possible grave consequences from further such "reckless" attacks.

Newspaper Article # 8:

The New York Times
September 28, 1954

TOLL PASSES 1,000 IN FERRY SINKING

Only 171 Survive of the 1,257 on Vessel Wrecked by Typhoon Off Japan

Tokyo, Tuesday, Sept. 28 –

Japanese and United States authorities counted today a grim death toll of more than 1,000 men, women and children drowned Sunday night when the train ferry Toya Maru turned over and sank off Hakodate on Japan's northernmost island of Hokkaido.

Officials of the National Railways, which operated the ferry between Hakodate and Aomori, on northern Honshu, announced this morning that there were 171 "confirmed survivors" of the typhoon disaster. The overloaded ship had 1,275 passengers, crew members and railway employees aboard. One thousand eighty-six persons were missing or dead at the latest count.

Perhaps 500, according to the national rural police on the scene of the sinking, were trapped inside the hull. The ship is now lying with her bottom out of the water about 100 yards from shore. A tragic procession of ambulances carried bodies from the beach, where the storm had flung them Many survivors, badly injured, were in a half dozen hospitals.

Of the dead and missing, fifty-seven were United States soldiers, their dependents, and Army employees, headquarters here said.

158

There was one known soldier survivor, Pfc. Frank Goedken, 21 years old, of Dubuque. Iowa.

Private Goedken, as far as he could tell in the tumult and confusion when the Toya Maru rolled over, was washed through a porthole. One of his arms was badly slashed, it was reported. But his condition was not considered critical. Beside military personnel, thirteen foreigners were believed to have been aboard the ferry. One was to known to have survived. He was Donald Orth, a missionary from Obihiro, on Hokkaido. Mrs. Emiko Champaigne, Japanese wife of Sgt. Charles Champaigne, was in a hospital in Hokkaido. Her husband's body was recovered.

Meanwhile, the Japanese Coast Guard and United States armed forces kept up the hunt for possible survivors or for bodies that may have floated out to sea.

Thirty-six vessels of the Japanese Maritime Safety Force, patrol boats, minesweepers and landing craft searched the waters near the scene of the disaster.

U.S. Ships to Join Search

Two United States Navy ships, and planes from four American bases in northern Japan, were scheduled to join the search today. High winds kept most aircraft from the skies.

The Japanese Coast Guard reported one freighter sunk and four others operated by the National Railways grounded during the storm. None carried passengers and the death toll was still uncertain. One hundred small sampans and fishing vessels were missing from ports of Hokkaido and northern Honshu, and believed sunk.

Meanwhile, inquiries were underway to fix responsibility for the train ferry disaster. The Hakodate Maritime Court was expected to hear witnesses from among the survivors. The Tokyo higher Maritime Court sent investigators to Hakodate.

There was at least some suspicion that negligence might have been to blame. The Central Meteorological Observatory here said all necessary warnings of the storm had been flashed to Hokkaido. The Tokyo newspaper Mainichi said editorially this morning that it was "strange" in view of this statement that the ferry sailing had not been cancelled.

Newspaper Articles # 9:

(Three articles is the same edition.)

Pacific Stars and Stripes

Tuesday, November 9, 1954:
UNOFFICIAL PUBLICATION OF THE UNITED STATES FORCES, FAR EAST
All-Japan Issue

2 MIGs SHOOT DOWN RB-29

U.S. Plane Crashes on Hokkaido; 1 Killed

Tokyo: A U.S. Air Force RB-29 crashed on Hokkaido at 11:53 a.m. Sunday after it was fired upon by two Russian-built MIG-type fighters. Crew members did not fire at the MIGs.

Both MIGs made two passes at the reconnaissance bomber, setting it afire.

The RB-29 was on a photo-mapping mission.

~~~~~~

Tokyo: Russian fighters shot down a U.S. RB-29 Superfort over the coast of northern Japan Sunday and the U.S. State Department immediately sent a protest to Moscow.

Ten of the eleven man crew of the U.S. photo-mapping plane parachuted to safety after bailing out into the open sea near Nemuro. The plane crashed at Bekkai, 30 miles west of Nemuro.

(unreadable photocopy) ... landed close to shore in the straits separating Hokkaido from two groups of Soviet-held islands.

162

Drowns Near Shore

His parachute had opened but he apparently drowned when only ten feet from shore. The only other injury reported was a small cut on the chin of one crewman.

In Washington, meanwhile, State Department Spokesman Joseph Reap said, "A protest has been sent to the American Embassy at Moscow" for relay to the Kremlin.

Reap said the RB-29 was on a routine mission along the east coast of Hokkaido when it was attacked. He said the bomber "did not at any time leave Japanese territory."

In Good Shape

An Air Force spokesman said the 10 men were in "good shape" at Yokota Air Base near Tokyo where they were flown late Sunday.

The incident market the sixth U.S. plane shot down by the Soviets in Far Eastern waters since November 6, 1951. At that time, a Navy patrol bomber disappeared off the coast of Siberia after an attack by Russian planes.

Two reconnaissance Superforts vanished in 1952 in the same area patrolled by the plane that crashed Sunday.

On July 29, 1953, an American B-50 patrol bomber vanished near Siberia after being attacked without warning by Russian fighters while over international waters 40 miles off the coast.

Tokyo: **Survivors OK**

The 10 survivors of the U.S. Air Force RB-29 shot down
by Russian-built MIGs over Hokkaido Sunday are in "excellent"
condition, Yokota AB Hospital authorities reported Monday.

The men were flown to their home station at Yokota AB,
near Tokyo, from Kenebetsu soon after Air Force trucks had
picked them up following the crash.

Newspaper Article Number 10:

(The photocopy of this article does not have the name of the newspaper or the date, but it was stapled with a few articles from the New York Times and the print looks the same so I think it was printed in the Times. The date is blurred but it looks like 1957 or 1958, and based on the text that seems right.)

~~~

First To Get The News

Yanks Eye Russ
32 Miles Away

This is another of a series of articles by Ed Koterba, Washington (D.C.) newspaperman, who is making a world tour of military installations to give the people back home a realistic picture of life in the outposts manned by United States servicemen.

by Ed Koterba

Wakkanai, Japan – On the world map, Wakkanai is just a little pip sitting on the far northwest coastline of Japan.

You stand on the beach and look north at the Russian hills just 32 miles away beyond the Soya Strait. And you know this is the end of the line.

The 460 men and officers of the United States Air Force who dwell here know it. But at the airmen's club, in the barracks, and at chow, they make kidding remarks about it.

NINETY SECONDS to live . . . That's what they used to say about this place," one fellow said. "That was when the top speed of jets was 600 miles an hour . . . Now it's about 45 seconds."

By cold calculation, he was about right - 45 seconds for the Russians to slip over the international line out there in the strait and drop a lethal load on this lonely outpost.

WE WERE sitting around the airmen's club talking idly about it when Walter Jarman, airman second class from Cockeville, Tennessee, piped up. "Man," he said, "you'd be surprised what a big hole I can dig in 45 seconds . . ."

These men have one purpose up in the hills above Wakkanai - to keep a radar eye on the Reds who, they figure, are glaring right back at them.

These modern-day sentinels seem to get a sort of kick out of boasting that they're probably farther away from American civiliz- ation than any other group of servicemen.

"How did you ever find out about this place?" asked Airman Second Class Elbert G. Anderson of Houston, Texas.

I told him I had heard about them at the Pentagon.

"You mean to tell me they actually know we exist?" he said, and everybody at the table laughed at this original gem of jovial sarcasm.

IT TOOK SOME getting to get here. The last stage was across the Island of Hokkaido in an L-120 four-place DeHavilland.

When we hove over the hills, to the coastline, the pilot, Captain Bruce Baker of Hagerstown, Maryland, nodded ahead to the land beyond the strait.

"That's Sakhalin," he said, "the island the Russians took from the Japanese in the last war."

Co-pilot Maj. A. W. Steward of Sheboygan, Wisconsin, turned around and said, "Should we keep going straight ahead? We've got plenty of gas to land over there."

I saw him wink at Baker, who made this understatement: "It'd make some big headlines back home . . . "

JUST THEN a bright orange flare shot up from the narrow beach of Wakkanai. "What's that?" I yelled.

"That's where we are going to land," said Capt. Baker, who was a fighter pilot in the China-Burma-India Theater back when.

I knew he was kidding again. Only this time he wasn't. That plane dipped right down into the sand and mushed to a stop with the sea water lapping at the wheels.

It's a naked feeling standing out there on the beach when you know that Siberia lies directly west of you, the Russian Kuriles directly east, and to the north those brown humps of Sakhalin.

It's a long way from home.

~~~~~~

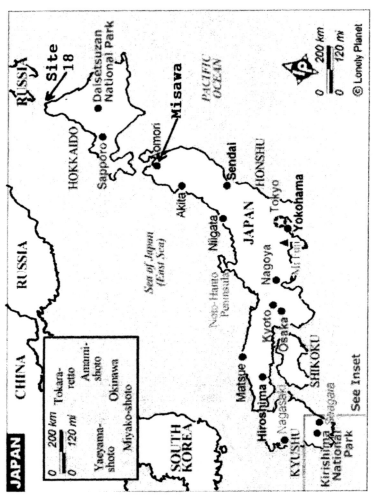

Site 18 at top right.

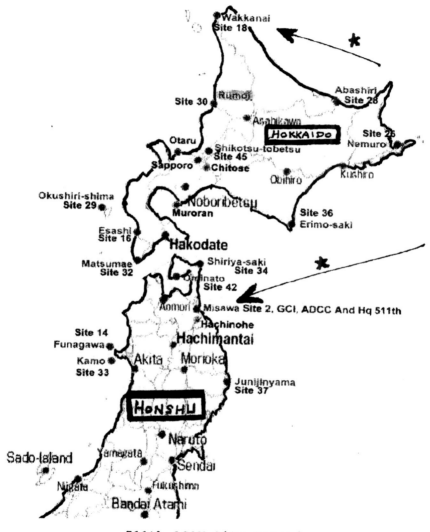

511th AC&W Site Locations

Site 18 Alumni

1952 and 1953

I was stationed at Site 18 for fifteen months in 1952 and 1953 and I knew about half of the 147 names listed below.

When I arrived, there were about 60 men stationed there, a fraction of the number to come in the following years.

After being an active US Air Force radar site for about ten years, Site 18 was transferred to the Japanese Air Defense Force (JADF), and they kept the name designation as their Site 18.

This book is only about some events during '52 and '53. What happened before and after is interesting but hard to pin down, and doesn't apply here. The site began around 1950, had an active and unusual military existence for some years, and then ceased to exist as an American radar detachment when it was turned over to the Japanese to continue the radar work.

The isolation, personnel, military informality and extreme winter weather ingrained Wakkanai in the minds of those who served there - time which ranged from a few weeks to 2 ½ years.

I decided to acknowledge those I found who were at 18 in 1952 and 1953 because I knew many of them. To acknowledge everyone from all years would be a book by itself.

Some of the 'Alumni' were short timers or were there before or after me, some jobs I remembered, some names and jobs I was told by others, and some names I could not match to jobs.

172

A 1952 'Table of Organization for an Early Warning Site' called for 2 officers and 58 enlisted men, much less than some hundreds stationed at Wakkanai years later. To illustrate, in 1957 (the exact date is unclear on the photocopy) a New York Times reporter visited the site and wrote of "460 men and officers at Wakkanai." That number probably included others not involved with radar but I do not have any firm knowledge or information on the personnel make-up so I'll stick with what I do know and the earlier time.

~~~

After this preamble is a list of 147 names, many deceased, that I compiled from memory and two main sources:

One source was an annual newsletter sent for years by Major Haines, the Commanding Officer of Site 18 for a few months in 1953. He kept in touch by mail with as many of 'Haines' Rangers' as he knew addresses. The nickname, Haines' Rangers, came from the horseback inspection shown in the short story.

More names were culled from those personnel, living and dead, found by members of the 511th AC&W Reunion Association.

There are many people to thank for the extensive work finding people stationed on the 511th radar sites. The biggest thanks go to Roger Wolf, the Membership Chairman, and Don Simmons, the Secretary, for their endless hours and efforts locating veterans of the sites. Many other members also contributed time searching.

For all their efforts, frustrations and results we are all grateful.

Dick Waldron

…Any errors listed are inadvertent and I take responsibility.

Site 18: 1952 and 1953

Oscar Aguilar - cook
Patrick Aki – air police
Max Aldrich – medic
Richard Anaka -
Adrian Anderson –
Joel Aragon – orderly room
Grover Ashcraft – radio op
Harry Aumiller - supply

Earl Bauman –
Bob Benning – radio op
Willard Bilsback (Lt.) -
Mark Bisby –
John Block -
Mel Boaz – radio op
Richard Bock -
Jesse (Blackie) Botello – cook
Harold Breckinridge – radio op - NCOIC
Ray Brokamp (Lt.) -
Murray Brown – radio maint
Gene Buckley – first sergeant / radar NCOIC

Gil Chance – radar op
Larry Charbonneau (Capt.) – Commanding Officer
Robert Cheney –
Al Chester -
Frank Ciarniello – radar op
Floyd (Flip) Claunch – Philco tech rep (civilian)
Ted Clay – radio op
Bob Cole – air police
Al Combs - supply
Dillon O. (Doc) Connell - medic
Dick Cox –
Jim Cox -

Gil Deese -
Bob Dietz – radio maint
Len Dillman – radio maint
George (Eddie) Dixon – radio op
Gerry Dress – radio maint
Ed Dube – radar maint
Tim Dunne – radio op

Merle (Cooler) Everett – motor pool

Paul Faulk – radio op
Ed Filesteele – radar op
Keith Fellerman (Lt.) -
Bill Foreman -
Art Freihoefer – radio maint
Sandy Friedman - radar maint

Gil Gaboury – motor pool
Reno Giuntoli – radio maint
Lee (Red) Goodwin – radar maint
Joe Gore – radar maint
Bob Gray – radio op
Mervin (Doc) Greenup - medic
Nick Gualillo – motor pool
Len Guzak – Philco Tech Rep (civilian)

Bill Haines (Maj.) – Commanding Officer
Sam Halburnian – radar op
G. Robert Hales (Lt.) -
Max Hancock –
Henry (Hank) Harashak – radar maint
Pfifer Hayes – cook
Jack Hedden -
Joe Hennessy - air police
Bob Herrin -
Aubrey Higgins – supply NCOIC
Tom Hilgeford -
Jack Hilyer – radar
Don (Dixie) Howell - radio op
Dick Huber – motor pool

John Jackson - supply
Glenn (Jake) Jacobsen – first sergeant / radio NCOIC
Arlie Jensen – air police
Don Johnson – air police
Ernest Jones -

Hilliard Leftwich -
Marv Lemanski -
Gordon Locklear – site maint
------ Logan – motor pool
Dick Loose (Lt.) – Commanding Officer
Dick Loveless – site maint
Charley Lovell -

Nat Mannino – radio maint
Paul Markovich – radar maint
Jack McCans – radar op
John McNicholas – radio maint
Roger Medford - radar
Sal Messina – radar op
George Miller –
Ira Miller -
George Mims – motor pool
Charley Moore -

John Nauman – radio op - NCOIC
Clarence Nauyalis –
Charlie Nocella – radar op
Royce Norton – motor pool

Tony Ocampo – radio maint - NCOIC
Hedy Ocampo - Japanese National - waitress
Ed (Ozzie) Osborne – radar op
Billy Outen – radio op
Einar Oxholm - radar op

Travis (Slim) Peninger – radio op
Harold Pfeiffer – radar maint
Bob (Pooch) Porche – radar op
Ray Porter –
John Pritchard –

Bob Reece – orderly room
Carl Rheinschmidt – radio op - NCOIC
Bob Riebling -
George (Red) Rife – radio op
Al Robinson – radio maint
Jim Robinson -
Harold Rothman – radio maint - NCOIC
Ron Royal -

John Sanders – motor pool
Reginald Schmidt -
Earl Seeley – radar maint
Al Setting – radio op
Paul Sheehan – radio maint
Carl Sidner -
Bill Sidwell – radio maint
Don Simmons – radar maint
Len Smalling – motor pool
----- **Smith** – orderly room
Bob Stehlik – radio op
George Strait -
Ravel Stroman – motor pool
Charles (Chuck) Swanson – radio op

Jessie Thompson – motor pool
Larry Ticer - cook
Carlos Tidwell - radio op
Paul Topping – radar maint
Bill Tucker – cook
Vernon Tucker -

Jack Vincent – radar maint – NCOIC
Paul Vise – radar maint
Les Vrieze – radar

Dick Waldron – radio op
Ed Waligorski – radar maint
-------- **Walker** – mess sergeant
Frank Watanabe – Japanese National - interpreter
Peggy Watanabe – Japanese National - waitress
Hugh (Meezuman) Waterman – radio maint
Ralph Weaver – radio op
Bill White – radar maint
Charles White -
Ray (Willie) Williams – radio op
Al Worthington – radio op

Harry (Yo-Yo) Youmans – radio op

~~~

Hokkaido

Japan is called Land of the Rising Sun;
therefore, could Hokkaido be called the

a) Land of the Gray Skies?
b) Land of the Daily Snowstorm?
c) Land of Zero Visibility?
d) Land of Rosy Cheeks?
e) Land of Hibachi Hand Warmers?
f) Land of Visible Breath?
g) Land of Whistling Wind?
h) Land of Driving Whiteouts?
i) Land of Tracked Vehicles?
j) Land of Short White Days?
k) Land of Long Black Nights?
l) Land of the Abominable Snowman?
m) Land of the Long Parka?
n) Land of Honeybucket Sam?
o) Land the Ainu Abandoned?
p) Land of the Stomping Feet?
q) Land of the Clapping Gloves?
r) Land of Faces Hooded In Parkas?
s) Land of Short Summers and Long Winters?
t) Land of Isolation?
u) Land of the Forgotten?
v) Land of Volunteered Visitors?
w) Land that American Southerners Hated?
x) Land that American Northerners Hated?
y) Land where Northerners Never Admit Discomfort?
z) Land of Lifelong Friends and Fond Memories?

...actually, all of the above. so desu.

an autobiography of sorts...

I was in Japan from June, 1952 to July, 1954 with 15 months at Site 18 at Wakkanai on Hokkaido and 10 months at Misawa AFB on Honshu.

I joined the Air Force in January, 1951 with five friends from Boston; had basic training at Lackland AFB in San Antonio and Nellis AFB in Las Vegas; was an office clerk and played for the Nellis baseball team; applied for radio operator school at Biloxi, Mississippi; and spent 32 weeks on C-Shift with classes from 6 P.M. until midnight, six nights a week.

From Biloxi I went to Site 18 as a ground radio operator. Later I got a ham radio license and after 15 months at Site 18 I was transferred to Misawa Air Base to start a MARS (ham radio) station. I did that and while at Misawa I was a reserve on the base football team. (We won our conference but lost the league championship game.) I later played on the Misawa baseball team.

My AF enlistment ended after Japan and on returning home I went to the University of Massachusetts where I got a degree in business. I then spent many years in data processing and computer sales, and after a layoff went into the water tower business. I also had unsuccessful self-employment efforts. When nothing significant happened I became a radio officer in the merchant marine at age 45 and went to sea for 13 years.

I sailed on various types of ships (about a dozen containerships, three oil research ships, an oil tanker, a roll-on, roll-off vehicle ship, a WWII Caine Mutiny-type cargo ship, and a fish factory-trawler). There were 60 Atlantic crossings, 15 Pacific crossings, 2 round-the-world trips, and 33 countries.

Since 'coming ashore,' I wrote a book in 1994 called "Futures 101: An Introduction To Commodity Trading" which is still in bookstores in 2005.

I married, had a son and daughter, and was widowed. I remarried, had two more sons and two grandchildren, and now live in Quincy, Massachusetts, happily married to Polly.

~~~~~~

Dick Waldron,   54 Monmouth Street,   Quincy, MA 02171-1048

Site 18 Order Form

Use this convenient order form to order additional copies
of
Site 18

Please Print:

Name_____

Address_____

City_____ **State**_____

Zip_____

Phone(**)**_____

_____ copies of book @ $19.95 each $ _____
Postage and handling @ $5.00 per book $ _____
MA residents add 6 % tax $ _____
Total amount enclosed $ _____

Make checks payable to Richard E. Waldron

Send to Richard E. Waldron
54 Monmouth Street • Quincy, MA 02171